CHRISTIANITY

in the

CROSSHAIRS

Real Life Solutions
Discovered in the Line of Fire

CHRISTIANITY

in the

CROSSHAIRS

Real Life Solutions
Discovered in the Line of Fire

BILL WILSON

Destiny Image® Publishers, Inc.
P.O. Box 310
Shippensburg, PA 17257-0310

"Speaking to the Purposes of God for This Generation
and for the Generations to Come"

ISBN 0-7684-2968-4

For Worldwide Distribution
Printed in the U.S.A.

This book and all other Destiny Image, Revival Press, MercyPlace, Fresh Bread, Destiny Image Fiction, and Treasure House books are available at Christian bookstores and distributors worldwide.

1 2 3 4 5 6 7 8 9 10 / 09 08 07 06 05 04

For a U.S. bookstore nearest you, call **1-800-722-6774**.
For more information on foreign distributors, call **717-532-3040**.
Or reach us on the Internet:
www.destinyimage.com

ENDORSEMENT

"I did not intend to read *Christianity in the Crosshairs* in one sitting, but I had no choice. Bill Wilson's story is that riveting. Get ready for a life-changing reading experience."

—Pat Williams
Senior Vice President
Orlando Magic

CONTENTS

FOREWORD

Every so often a book comes along that captures the heart and subdues the imagination. A book that makes you feel like it's about you. A book that captures the human experience and makes you feel that you too can achieve your goals. This is one of those books.

The issue of leadership has been the subject of thousands of years of study, review, and investigation. The nature of leadership is as complex as any attempt to define it, yet the pursuit of leadership is inherent and basic to human nature. I believe leadership is a personal issue. That is, it is the result of an individual's personal discovery that ignites an inner spark of faith, conviction, passion, and a sense of destiny and obligation to humanity.

Bill Wilson, in this book, proves that very point. This book is not about theory, but is a journal of the process of how the Creator makes a man a leader. The process is not unique, but for all who desire to be leaders, it is necessary. This is why this book is so important. It presents a life-learning program, and is a road map for all of us to learn once again that success in life is not a gift but a result.

The creation of mankind in the biblical text implies through the use of the word *dominion*, that the purpose of God in creating man was that he exercise a measure of delegated power and authority over the earth. This is the foundation of leadership. When you discover your area of dominion, then you have discovered your personal leadership.

In this context, leadership potential resides in every human. However, the exercise of this leadership potential is different in each person. The nature of leadership seems to be released through the mode of influence, through inspiration.

Drawing on his rich life experiences and a past that seems to be taken from a movie script, Bill Wilson presents the challenge of true leadership and provides the power and principles of true leadership to overcome these challenges. This work has captured the awesome responsibility required for one to exercise his or her God-given potential. His focus on the leadership ability in each of us provides a unique perspective for both women and men, helping us to understand the critical nature of the use and effective development of leadership potential. This is a must-read for all who desire to know the truth about their hidden leadership potential and maximize this dormant power. Read on and explore a fresh perspective on an age-old subject.

His invitation for you and me to come to the secret place in God as leaders and draw courage and resolve from His grace is a graphic illustration that makes this book unique and different from the many quick-fix leadership books that clutter our shelves.

This is an excellent book for the leader who may be discouraged, and who may have lost the vision. It is a manual and source of inspiration for the aspiring leader who dares to step out and take up the challenge of becoming the leader they were born to be. I challenge you to embrace the wisdom of this book and watch your passion emerge or re-emerge in your leadership.

—Dr. Myles E. Munroe
Bahamas Faith Ministries International
Nassau, Bahamas

INTRODUCTION

It was about 9:30 pm on a clear March night in 2003 as I was walking along the East River in Brooklyn. I have, in the past, come to this area to minister to the homeless men and take photos for the ministry newsletter. As I was walking through a vacant lot taking photos, two men approached me from behind. They grabbed me in a suffocating chokehold so fast that I had no time to react. "Gimme your wallet!" was all I heard. As a rule, I don't carry it while I'm out in dangerous places. They became infuriated when I told them I didn't have my wallet. So they went through my pockets for anything of value, taking my camera and watch. As I was striving to remain conscious and fight, I heard, "Just kill him...just kill him."

Something like a steel pipe was forced into my mouth. I really didn't realize it was a gun until I heard the distinctive sound of the hammer of the gun releasing. That means the guy pulled the trigger, but the gun misfired.

I struggled even more to get free. Why shouldn't I? I was a dead man anyway. I remember saying "Jesus help me." As I tried to twist to the left and down to get loose, he pulled the trigger again and it felt like my head exploded. The bullet ripped through the left side of my face. I collapsed to the ground. The men went running. Since I had been shot in the head, they figured I was dead.

I don't know how long I lay on the ground, but I remember touching my face and knew I was losing a lot of blood. I had to move quickly or I'd bleed to death. Somehow I made it back to the van where my cell phone was. Blood was spurting straight out of the side of my face. I called 911 and then called someone from the ministry to meet me at the hospital. I could only get out a few words: "I've been shot."

I knew I couldn't wait for an ambulance. I raced to the nearest hospital, which just happens to be one of the roughest hospitals in the city. They admitted me immediately and did a three-hour emergency surgery to repair the damage from the bullet on the inside and outside of my face. It was a 15-minute ride. You can think about a lot of things in 15 minutes, especially when you're bleeding to death.

They left me for dead but God raised me up for the entire world to see. He has allowed a small boy, unwanted by his own mother, to speak literally all over the world and on platforms that I would never have dreamed I would be on. Because of these platforms, I have, through the years, met people just like *you*, who have a dream and vision in their hearts to reach their cities for Christ and to do something effective for the Kingdom.

I have counseled, prayed, and cried with a lot of you and hopefully encouraged you in this quest. And as a result, many of you have encouraged me to put my thoughts and life-principles into book form. I always knew I should do it, but, to be quite honest, I have struggled with writing just "another book" on leadership, motivation, or "ministry secrets." As I come to my 35th anniversary of living and ministering in the inner city, I believe that I have learned some valuable principles while literally "in the line of fire" that will encourage, motivate, and hopefully, provoke you into action.

I believe that all of our God-given desires and visions have always been "in the crosshairs" of the enemy. He wants to destroy the vision that God has given you. I know at various times in my life, he tried to destroy mine. But we all know that he is crafty in his attempts. The way he does that is sometimes not always as obvious as a shooting. Sometimes it is the little things that keep wearying and discouraging you. The Scripture says, "Where there is no vision, the people perish" (Prov. 29:18a, KJV). Most Christians apply that to the lives of the lost, but I would like you to apply it to your life, as a believer. Maybe you have a God-given vision for doing something for Him. You are struggling with it…maybe you have given up on it and now feel guilty for doing so. I have been where you are. In spite of all the weapons of discouragement that have come my way, I am still standing and declaring that *you* too can persevere and make a difference!

I believe these principles will help you get there! They have for me.

—Bill Wilson

PART 1

PRINCIPLES FROM
THE LAND OF ONO

But it so happened, when Sanballat heard that we were re-building the wall, that he was furious and very indignant, and mocked the Jews. And he spoke before his brethren and the army of Samaria, and said, "What are these feeble Jews doing? Will they fortify themselves? Will they offer sacrifices? Will they complete it in a day? Will they revive the stones from the heaps of rubbish—stones that are burned?" Now Tobiah the Ammonite was beside him, and he said, "Whatever they build, if even a fox goes up on it, he will break down their stone wall." Hear, O our God, for we are despised; turn their reproach on their own heads, and give them as plunder to a land of captivity! Do not cover their iniquity, and do not let their sin be blotted out from before You; for they have provoked You to anger before the builders. So we built the wall, and the entire wall was joined together up to half its height, for the people had a mind to work (Neh. 4:1-6, NKJV).

The story of Nehemiah is a compelling story of one man's triumph in the face of relentless criticism, horrific opposition, insidious undermining of his authority, and disheartening hostility to every decision he made and every deed he initiated. His words and his work fly in the face of this band of disgruntled and envious detractors. Empowered by his vision for this enormous task, he stands his ground with a faith that fortifies his soul. His faith in God's plan and provisions are stronger than the enemy's attempt to bring him down. As those around him struggle with doubt and constant criticism, Nehemiah takes the ultimate step of sacrifice, standing with those who have committed their lives and resources to this great enterprise. Day by day, he illustrates this commitment with a sacrifice that serves others in the midst of mounting opposition.

Any task worth accomplishing will require great sacrifice on the part of those who seek to be involved.

In the midst of the daily and somewhat mundane chores that must be done to accomplish the overall task, there will always be the temptation to take shortcuts in the effort to minimize cost, energy, and time. A true leader knows that if he is to be successful and lay a good foundation for following generations, he must build a foundation that endures the test of time. There can be no shortcuts, and he must always build with his eye upon the future.

Before a plan can be successfully shaped and implemented, it must first be contemplated through the process of strategic thinking. The plans that define the work originate from a mind that mattered. Behind every great work there are timeless thoughts and creative concepts being formed in the mind of the leader, enabling him to develop a plan that will successfully accomplish the task set before him.

At the turn of every corner, you always run the risk of bumping your nose on the face of the opposition. There has never been any lack of naysayers who are there to offer their devious thoughts and discouraging words, as illustrated through Nehemiah's example. But these challenges are also a part of the process. They are the "resistance that refines you" as you are engaged in the process of fulfilling your dreams.

In the next five chapters, you will visit the land of ONO. In that land you will discover powerful principles that will enable you to accomplish your own journey. They are not just principles. They are truths that have been forged into the core of my being and have enabled me to accomplish the great tasks that the Father has given me. It is not enough to study them and memorize them. You will be pressed by the challenges of your life and hopefully, you will allow these principles to also be merged into the fabric of your own life. In that way, these static truths will become living principles in your own life.

When you decide to work for change and commit yourself to accomplishing God's purposes wherever you are, people will come against you. When facing opposition, you can choose either to become more dedicated or more discouraged. It's your choice.

—Bill Wilson

All the strength and force of man comes from his faith in things unseen. He who believes is strong; he who doubts is weak. Strong convictions precede great actions.

—James Freeman Clarke

The only limit to our realization of tomorrow will be our doubts of today; let us move forward with strong and active faith.

—Franklin D. Roosevelt

CHAPTER 1

A FAITH THAT FORTIFIES

Once, while I was speaking at a conference in Singapore, a young man approached me. I could tell that he wanted to talk. After introducing himself, he told me this sad story that is all too common:

> "I really feel like I can make a difference in this city. I've watched you in New York, I've read the books, I've watched you on television, and I've seen all the videos. The last time when you were here, I felt that I needed to sell out and be completely dedicated to what I'm doing for God. When I got home, I was very excited, but my family looked at me and said, 'Oh, no! You can't do that! We have other plans for your life.'"

Several years later in the United States, I was speaking at another conference. One of the people in attendance at that conference, a leader in his church, went back all excited about soul winning and reaching his city for God. He enthusiastically submitted a proposal at one of his church board meetings—a plan that included reaching out to the lost kids in his town. At the end of his presentation, the board members promptly shot down his proposal. The horrified board members declared, "*Oh, no.* We're not going to have those kinds of kids in our church."

While speaking at a convention on missions, I met another young man who had felt the call of God on his life. He told me that he sensed the need to go to the mission field. He felt confident that his life was going to move in that direction. When he went back home and excitedly shared his vision with his wife, she forcefully protested, "*Oh, no.* We're not moving to the mission field—not me, not our two kids, and not you."

CONFRONTING THE ENEMY OF "OH NO"

Three people, three stories—people very close to them had rejected the call of God on their lives. That rejection led to abandoning the call. Sometimes, even our most intimate friends are transformed into a voice that contradicts the Voice. How many people every day reject God's call because of the poison of misdirected influence? Those who have influence in our lives—fathers, mothers, wives, pastors, friends—these are the ones who should be encouraging the divine call on our life, not exterminating it.

The above scenario isn't a new one. It's been happening ever since Adam and Eve first listened to the "other voice" in the Garden—the voice of the serpent. There will always be many voices competing with the sound of the one Voice. A wise man or woman will learn to discern the sound of other voices and reject them in favor of listening to and obeying the voice of Father. When we choose to listen to the other voices rather than doing what is right, we reduce ourselves to the "minimum rather than the maximum" and we will never be able to rise to the heights of the high calling of God on our lives. If you are ever going to make something significant of life, then you must learn how to face down your enemies.

> But it so happened, when Sanballat heard that we were rebuilding the wall, that he was furious and very indignant, and mocked the Jews. And he spoke before his brethren and the army of Samaria, and said, "What are these feeble Jews doing? Will they fortify themselves? Will they offer sacrifices? Will they complete it in a day? Will they revive the stones from the heaps of rubbish—stones that are burned?" Now Tobiah the Ammonite was beside him, and he said, "Whatever they build, if even a fox goes up on it, he will break down their stone wall."...
>
> Now it happened when Sanballat, Tobiah, Geshem the Arab, and the rest of our enemies heard that I had rebuilt the wall, and that there were no breaks left in it (though at that time I had not hung the doors in the gates), that Sanballat and Geshem sent to me, saying, "Come, let us meet together among the villages in the plain of **Ono**" (Neh. 4:1-3; 6:1-2, NKJV).

Nehemiah 6:2 holds the key: "Come, let us meet together among the villages in the plain of *Ono.*" The response of the young man's family in Singapore was, "*Oh no*, we have other plans for your life." One of the board members said, "*Oh no*, we're not going to have those kinds of kids in our church." When the young man's wife learned he was thinking about going on the mission field she declared, "Oh no, you're not going to do that." Nothing every changes, does it? Man will always be troubled by the voices from the land of *Oh, no*!

Any time you begin building something—a home, a family, a church, or a life, whatever it is that you decide to build—people (usually well-meaning people) will come against you for a variety of reasons. No one likes change and when someone comes around with a vision that will disturb their comfortable, secure life, they will automatically respond, "Oh no"!

Since you are reading this, you are probably aware of some well-meaning people who have discouraged you and spoken negative, hurtful words about your vision and call. You are not alone. Everyone who stands up to resist the flow of normal life will face opposition. That is the nature of swimming upstream. When you face these discouraging and critical words, what should you do?

WELL-MEANING DRAGONS

I learned a long time ago that there are many well-intentioned dragons that periodically rear up their ugly heads creating problems for people. When I first went to New York City and started the Sunday school, some of these dragons decided that what I was doing wasn't worthy of support. These detached bureaucrats decided that Sunday school wasn't necessary in the inner city, so they did their best to shoot down my vision. I find it amazing that those who sit on the sidelines seem to be so *qualified* to make decisions for those risking their lives as they play the game. It is so much easier to tell people what they should or should not be doing as opposed to getting out there and doing it yourself. These Monday morning quarterbacks might feel secure and smug in the advice they dish out to others, but one thing is clear: they will never know the sense of joy and fulfillment that comes from getting your hands dirty as you work to fulfill the dream God has given you.

These armchair colonels are all gone now. They've retired, put on their Bermuda shorts and are playing shuffleboard somewhere in Florida. That's how the careers of bureaucrats usually end. Imagine what could have happened had they lived their lives differently. I don't respect people simply because of the position they occupy. I respect them for who they are and what they've done and the principles for which they stand. From my own life, I know that who you are dramatically influences what you do. Your inner values will determine your outward victories.

When you commit your life to change, entrusting yourself to build God's kingdom wherever you are, people will come against you. I know that firsthand, having faced many a "Doubting Thomas" and "Gloomy Gus" in my day. In the face of these detractors, I've dedicated my life to making a difference in some very unusual parts of the world—parts that most of us would not choose. The conflicts we face never seem to change. Whether it's in a small group or a large ministry, individually or collectively, opposition always rises up against the work of God. Here is a key that I have discovered. When facing opposition, you either become more dedicated or more discouraged. It's your choice. You can let resistance pull you down or you can face it straight on and rise above its toothless growl. Robert Savage, the famed surgeon, said, "You can measure a man by the opposition it takes to discourage him."[1]

Cynics and skeptics will always be around. I know that it's easy to let discouraging words and criticism hurt you and destroy your ministry. These gangs of troublemakers will never disappear; so, if you think they will, think again. Someone else will always reappear to criticize either you or the ministry that you're doing. The choice is yours—will you take your stand publicly on behalf of God's purposes, or shrink back into a web of anonymity and disgrace?

VOICES OF MOCKERY

Nehemiah's hecklers mocked both him and the Jews as they questioned them, insinuating the wall could never be restored. The shrewdly formulated questions were directed straight at Nehemiah and his companions' ability to get the job done. They hoped that this seed of doubt, shrewdly placed in their minds, would reduce their confidence in themselves.

Those who have opposed me in the past have used this same devious way of attempting to break down my confidence and convictions. It is an old trick that has been used many, many times. Likewise, your critics will question your ability not only to do the work but even your ability to hear God! I fought brutal criticism and censuring when I first went to New York: "You're not able to do that; nobody else has ever done it." In light of these caustic words, I find it interesting that nobody else in the history of the United States has been able to do what's been done in New York. It's never happened before and nothing like it has happened since. Not to the magnitude of what we're doing and not in the type of neighborhoods we've done it. But like Donald Rumsfeld said, "If you are not criticized, you may not be doing much."[2]

Believe me, I understand the root of their skepticism. It's perfectly natural that people would doubt that an unqualified nobody like me would ever accomplish anything. But God had a different idea. In fact, Paul made it clear that God's methods are different than ours. He likes to use *unskilled labor* to get His job done. As Paul said, "and the base things of the world and the despised God has chosen, the things that are not, that He may nullify the things that are" (1 Cor. 1:28, NASB). When God has a different idea, you'd better move aside because God doesn't wait for anyone. When He gets something in His head, He will get the job done, in spite of the disapproving ones.

I know a young, single woman who felt God was directing her to be a missionary to Haiti. Well-meaning people offered their opinions questioning her sanity or something worse. She used to be a fashion model. They didn't think she was cut out for the missionary lifestyle. They went on to say that it would be too hard for someone like her. That's a natural, normal response from people who do little or nothing for the Kingdom. They never stepped out into the deep waters and prevent others from doing it. However, she was smart enough to recognize the source of the discouraging words and didn't let it affect her. In the face of the opposition, she went to Haiti and once there, she became more dedicated instead of more discouraged.

If you are affected by how others perceive you (and unfortunately perception is 90 percent of life and is all that most of us seek), then you'll be limited in what you accomplish in life. Perception is not a bad thing as long as it's accurate. However, if it's inaccurate, there are problems. The tactic of creating false perception was used to try and get Nehemiah to come down off the wall and stop doing what he knew needed to be done. His cynical commentators asked him, "Do you really think you can do this? Do you actually think you can restore the wall?"

I know many people that have had great desires in life and have set out to do some wonderful things. But when the reality sets in, the truth of the matter is that you do get tired of the struggle—trying to raise money and trying to live in a place that's not overly friendly—whether on the mission field or in their own country. All it takes is one person to interject a word of criticism and then that thought can become a weapon of pain.

THE DEDICATED PERSEVERE—THE DISCOURAGED RESIGN

When I first started encountering great challenges in this work—violence on the streets, traveling every week to raise funds, training staff workers, et cetera—I persevered in the face of these challenges. I still don't feel like much of a fundraiser and I wonder if it's even my responsibility, but I continue to do it, because there is no one else. Every week for more than 20 years, I've stepped on a plane, traveling across the world, because that's what it takes. I take care of my responsibilities here in New York City and during the week, I will jump on a plane to go preach and take an offering, hoping that it is enough to fill the need for the coming week. I could get very discouraged, wondering how long I will have to do this. I could give in to the doubt and despair, but instead, I've chosen to increase the level of dedication rather than give in to the fatigue produced by the continuous pressures of the work. Ronald Reagan said it best with these words: "A leader, once convinced that a particular course of action is the right one, must...be undaunted when the going gets tough."[3]

A missionary and his two sons were ministering in Northern India when an anti-Christian mob trapped them in their car and set it on fire. When the missionary and his sons tried to get out, the mob shot arrows at them, preventing their escape. They were burned alive inside that car, persevering to their deaths in spite of the opposition, although they eventually died.

Scores of wonderful missionaries have served the purposes of God on the foreign field in valiant ways. They're great people with a great calling on their lives, but the most common reason missionaries quit is not because the work is too hard. It's because they get discouraged, lose sight of the original vision, and give up in despair.

I know of one situation in which missionaries took a famous personality to an impoverished African village. This well-known minister was going there hoping to raise money in the United States to help feed the malnourished children. When he arrived and saw their condition, he commented that their swollen bellies weren't swollen enough! Sad, isn't it? That day, the missionaries God sent to that village became very discouraged because of the crass, hardened heart of this minister.

When I first arrived in New York, I remembered thinking, "This is going to be great. We're working with kids in the ghetto. We're going to do this. We're going to do that. This is going to be the greatest thing since sliced bread." It didn't take long until I had that proverbial rude awakening. I really thought that with the results we were experiencing—all the miraculous things that were happening, all the kids coming to Christ and the lives being changed and families being put back together again—certainly this would motivate people to get involved. I had no trouble believing that when others saw the fruit of my effort, they would immediately jump on the bandwagon to help. Well, silly me. It did not quite happen that way. As the reality began to dawn, I came to the shocking realization that it would require of me a fulltime effort—twenty-four hours a day, seven days a week, and most of the time it was just God and me.

Criticism is like dripping water. The annoyance gradually wears on you making you irritable as it breaks down your resistance and leaves you fully discouraged. The source of discouragement comes in many packages. People with hidden agendas and impure motives will discourage you…if you let 'em! Nevertheless, God has given you the power to choose dedication over discouragement and resolution over resignation.

GET READY TO BUILD GOD'S VISION

Do you know what God has called you to do? Do you think you can do it? Nehemiah thought he could. Philippians 4:13 declares, "I can do all things through Christ who strengthens me" (NKJV). Some days you may think you are standing all alone. On other days, you might think that no one really cares if you fail or succeed. At times you might feel like you are fighting all by yourself. However, that's not the case. God is with you just as He was with Nehemiah. The sign of His presence might not always be visible, but I can assure you that He is there and He is battling on your behalf. He is there, setting ambushes against those who are speaking evil of you. He is there, sometimes in the shadows, working out the victory that you need. While He is doing His part, all that He asks is that you trust Him. It won't always be easy but it is that naked trust in the face of unbelievable odds that will bring the ultimate success.

You can do whatever God has called you to do! Overcoming opposition and building a dream isn't just for the Christian "marines" (the brave, the few, and the proud). It's for every believer who will dedicate himself or herself to Christ. How bad do you want to do it? Beware of continually looking at the price tag— "How much is this thing going to cost me?" Well, there is a price tag on everything. Success always has a price tag. Sometimes it is pretty high. It'll cost you criticism, opposition, and discouragement. Vince Lombardi, maybe one of the greatest motivators of all time, said, "The price of success is hard work, dedication to the job at hand, and the determination that whether we win or lose, we have applied the best of ourselves to the task at hand."[4] If you are to succeed in life, it will cost you something. You will always have your critics, but if you sit by the river long enough, you will inevitably see your enemies float by.

However, the good news is that none of these will last forever. Eventually, your detractors will get tired of howling in the wind and go back to their caves. What will last are the changed lives and a new hope instilled in others, because you made a decision to make a difference in your generation. Make a decision today to:

- outlast the opposition
- persevere through the pain
- snub the scorn

As you commit yourself to the building of your dream, you must be willing to look beyond the conflict to the Christ, who empowers you to build His vision, which will last forever!

LIFE PRINCIPLES IN THE CROSSHAIRS:

- **Voices from the Land of "Oh, no!"**
  No one likes change and when someone comes around with a vision that will disturb their comfortable, secure life they will automatically respond, "Oh no!"

Everyone who stands up to resist the flow of life will face opposition. That is the nature of swimming upstream, and everyone who succeeds in life has learned to resist the visually impaired.

- **Well-meaning dragons**
  When you decide to work for change and commit yourself to build God's new thing wherever you are, people will come against you. When facing opposition, you can either choose to become more dedicated or more discouraged. It's your choice.

- **Voices of mockery**
  Believe me, I understand the root of their skepticism. It's perfectly natural that people would doubt that an unqualified nobody like me would ever accomplish anything. But God had a different idea. In fact, Paul made it clear that God's methods are different than ours. He likes to use *unskilled labor* to get His job done.

- **The dedicated persevere—the discouraged give up.**
  The source of discouragement comes in many packages. People with hidden agendas and impure motives will discourage you...if you let 'em! Nevertheless, God has given you the power to choose dedication over discouragement and resolution over resignation.

- **Get ready to build God's vision.**
  You can do whatever God has called you to do! Overcoming opposition and building a dream isn't just for the Christian "marines" (the brave, the few and the proud). It's for every believer who will dedicate himself or herself to Christ.

I'm not some great man of power and faith. I'm a regular guy that often runs scared too. However, I think that faith without works is dead (James 2:17), so I don't sit around expecting God to drop what's needed out of the sky. Nevertheless, an issue of faith dictates the need I have to cross the line in the first place.

—Bill Wilson

Take the first step in faith. You don't have to see the whole staircase, just take the first step.

—Dr. Martin Luther King Jr.

Faith is the strength by which a shattered world shall emerge into the light.

—Helen Keller

Money is like manure; it's not worth a thing unless it's spread around encouraging young things to grow.

—Thornton Wilder

CHAPTER 2

A SACRIFICE THAT SERVES

As the crowd of critics stood facing Nehemiah, they served up the question concerning a key part of Jewish worship in the Temple: "Will they offer sacrifices?" (Neh. 4:2, NKJV) Behind the question was the subtle suggestion of doubt thrown in Nehemiah's direction. "Who's going to pay for it?"

Does that sound familiar? It is one of the old tools of the horde of hecklers who always stand in opposition to any new idea. It is such an easy volley hit into the court of those who would serve the Lord. Often when you get a God idea (notice I said God, not good), someone always asks, "Where's the money?" When it's God, it's usually not already in the budget so the money has to come from somewhere. Let me explain something: "Sometimes it's just not in the budget!" Just because something is not in the budget does not mean that it is not a God idea, and it doesn't necessarily mean that we cannot do it. "Well, where are we going to get the money?" they continue to probe. Figure it out. If the vision is from God, He'll provide the money! This is the key. It is not a key to be used for reckless activity that is not God-inspired. The money always follows the ministry. It always has and it always will. The first step in the process is to make very sure that your orders have the seal of God upon them. Then, it is in that holy confidence that you can trust God for the finances to support the mission.

This is where faith and hard work meet. Faith doesn't sit in a foxhole hoping the enemy goes away. Faith steps out of the foxhole and moves forward, trusting that Father will be will him. Step out in the faith you have *now* and watch how God works with you to accomplish His plan. Remember that it's God's agenda, not yours. Don't worry about the money—that's God's deal. Your deal is to simply trust and obey, as the old hymnist wrote.

YOUR FAITH ATTRACTS GOD'S BLESSING

I've learned in ministry that once you reach people's hearts, you can then reach their wallets. Often, people get it just the opposite and say, "Well, when we get enough money...." It's like getting married. "Well, when I'm ready, then...." How do you get ready to spend your life with someone? You tell me, because I'd like to know.

The issue is that the reward follows the faith, not vice versa. If you don't step out in faith, responding to the call of the Lord, then you cannot expect to receive the blessing of the Lord. Father blesses faith, not presumption. Dorothy Parker said, "If you want to know what God thinks of money, just look at the people He gave it to."[1] Abraham was a blessed man but his blessings flowed from his faith and willingness to leave the place of security and go to a place of obscurity. This scheme of satan has done more to keep the work of the Kingdom undone than anything else. Delays are disastrous when God says, "Now." If you're not doing it now, you won't do it later. This same group of couch potatoes argues over what color to paint the bathrooms and other inane matters. I've seen churches split right down the middle because they had church people trying to construct the church! Somebody, it seems, always has something negative to say. "Well, who's going to pay for this?" "Can't do it, there's no money."

When I went to New York, I had nothing; nothing, that is, except a willingness to obey God and go. I obeyed though I had nothing. I have watched over the years as God has faithfully blessed every new step that I have taken.

When we were trying to get our first building, we had only $98.16 in the ministry account. The down payment for the building was $25,000, a very large sum when you have only $98.16. The easiest thing to do would have been to say that we couldn't do it. Faith and determination will find a way to remove obstacles and complete the plan.

Now, we're purchasing an entire city block that encompasses five office buildings. It's been 20 years, but everything is relative, isn't it? A long time ago, it was only $25,000 that we were trusting in God for. Now, it's a couple of million dollars here and a few more million dollars there. It took a measure of faith 20 years ago to step out and buy that building when we had only $98.16. It's the same today; it still takes faith to step out. The amount is larger but the degree of faith is the same.

APPLY THE FAITH YOU HAVE RIGHT NOW

What I learned during those days was to take the measure of faith that I had and apply it to the situation where I was at that point in time. I learned that I couldn't wait until I thought I had enough faith to step out. I stepped out and saw my faith grow and stretch into the measure of faith that God could use for the situation at hand. James Freeman Clarke, a 19th-century theologian, said, "All the strength and force of man comes from his faith in things unseen. He who believes is strong; he who doubts is weak. Strong convictions precede great actions."[2] It has always been the power of faith that has enabled me to go to the next phase of God's work for my life.

Don't say to yourself, "When I have enough faith, I'll step out and do what God commands." Instead, go with what you've got. It only takes a mustard seed of faith to build something great in God's kingdom:

> And the apostles said to the Lord, "Increase our faith." So the Lord said, "If you have faith as a mustard seed, you can say to this mulberry tree, 'Be pulled up by the roots and be planted in the sea,' and it would obey you" (Luke 17:5-6, NKJV).

As you step out in obedience, your faith will continue to grow. That is one of the dynamic truths about faith. It is like our muscles; it grows with exercise. The reverse is also true; it atrophies and becomes stiff with inactivity. As the faith continues to grow, you can then apply it to the situations that are confronting you. You'll grow in the process as well, but if you don't take the first initial step, you'll never get anywhere. That's why so many people are immobilized in their faith; they don't step out. "You don't understand!" people say. "We have the house payment, the car payment, and the payment on our MasterCard." Most of you need to cut up the credit cards anyway because they'll rule you. They will become your master. That's why they call it "MasterCard."

When I first went to New York, we rented a few buses and we tried to buy a few. We also had some drug dealers that were paid $20 a week to drive those buses. Oh, I can almost hear those critics now. "Don't tell me that you pay drug addicts to drive those buses!" We don't talk about that too often because people tend to freak out when they hear we pay drug dealers. We were forced to do it because most church people won't come and do it.

For a week we had unsaved drug addicts and dealers handing out flyers about our services before we started. We were telling the kids on the streets that if they wanted to go to Sunday school they needed to stand outside at nine o'clock in the morning, and we would pick them up with the bus. The first day we started Metro Sunday School, 1,010 kids showed up. That's interesting isn't it? An act of faith will always produce a bundle of blessing.

IS THIS FOR REAL?

I can remember the time that we received a call from a church in Toronto that had five buses that they wanted to donate to the ministry. We thought this was such a great answer to prayer because we couldn't afford to buy any at the time. So we jumped on this unbelievable deal. See, there's always a way around your problems. Have you ever noticed that? If you want it bad enough there's always a way to figure it out. They said they would give us five buses. I was 31 years old, just past the stupid stage of life and entering the quasi-moronic stage. However, not all my stupidity was gone. I had to realize the hard way that often when a church gives something away, it's junk. That's another undeniable principle of church life: You are only offered what nobody wants. That's exactly why they were giving them away. If they were any good, they'd keep them for themselves.

Naturally, this happens in the middle of winter because everything I do is in the middle of winter. So I rounded up a team and we drove up to Toronto to get the buses. Typical of church buses, they won't start. Then when they do start, they won't stop. You know the drill, one thing after another.

The bus I drove back was missing the front windshield. It had a windshield wiper, but it didn't have a windshield. I drove it like that for six months in New York City. That's why I love New York, you make your own rules. It really was funny. Every time it rained, I just turned on the windshield wiper. The kids thought it was the funniest thing they'd ever seen. "Yeah, Pastor Bill, you go."

Are You Willing to Sacrifice?

So, what's the point of all this? Money will always be a point of contention, but you must decide what you want. Are you willing to sacrifice? I like the way it reads in Nehemiah 4:2: "Will they offer sacrifices?" (NKJV) Is somebody willing to step up to the plate and make the sacrifice? It's the story of Zerubbabel all over again (see Ezra 4-5). God said to set the foundation of the temple. Zerubbabel said there was no money. However, God said to set the foundation. Just set the foundation! Step out. Get out of the box! Move out and do what He told you to do. Oswald Chambers wrote, "Faith is deliberate confidence in the character of God whose ways you may not understand at the time."[3] Your ability to get out of the box is in direct proportion to the understanding you have of the God who has called you to step out.

Stepping out into the unknown is always scary. It's scary because we like to have all of our ducks in a row before we venture forth. It's scary because no one likes leaving the known and launching out to face the unknown. Faith is not contingent on our ability to make things happen by our human ingenuity or abilities. Faith is subject to the powers that have called upon us to act. Faith does not mean that we are free of fear; it means that we move out in spite of our fears.

I'm just like you. When I first started, I was scared to death. Even now, 20 years later, I still run scared. I'd be less than honest if I said I didn't. I'm responsible for a lot of people and a lot of families. I'm responsible to put food on lots of tables every week, pay salaries, and I take that responsibility very seriously.

The weight of that responsibility is why I travel every week to raise the funds necessary to stay afloat. It would be real easy for me to say, "Well, bless God, I'm going to believe God that I'm not going to have to travel. I'm going to cancel all my meetings." I'm probably not going to do that. Faith does move mountains but it doesn't mean we stop pushing.

Last year, when Metro was doing the Christmas present project, *Operation: Holiday Hope,* I was on television during September, October, November, and December trying to raise money to get 40,000 Christmas presents for the kids. That many Christmas presents represent lots of money that can't come out of the budget; it must come from somewhere else. Therefore, I stood by the promise of God and declared that by faith it will happen. Nevertheless, I still have some responsibility to ensure that it does. I take action based on that faith.

While I was fighting tuberculosis, the doctors told me that I shouldn't travel, but I did anyway. This wasn't one of the brighter things I've done in recent memory, and I don't recommend it, but it caused me to wonder: Is this faith? I don't know, but I've asked myself that question a lot since then. Nevertheless, I keep moving forward. I keep doing the things I know that I must do. I keep trusting the words that I hear from the invisible realm, trying to work them out in this realm. That same faith had to be exercised when I had hepatitis, when I was shot in the face and when dealing with all the other challenges I have had to face.

It's not easy for me to share this with you. I've said it before and I'll say it again. I'm not some great man of power and faith. I'm a regular guy that often runs scared too. However, I know that, as James put it, faith without works is dead (see James 2:17). Therefore, I don't sit around expecting God to drop what's needed out of the sky and into my lap. Faith causes me to rise up and cross the line of security into the land of insecurity as I seek to do what the Father has called me to do.

It's Time to Step Out in Faith

In one of the Indiana Jones episodes, Indiana was standing in front of a deep chasm needing to get across before the bad guys got to him. Only one problem—there was no bridge to get him across. He was told to step out anyway, even though there was nothing on which to place his feet. When he finally put his foot forward and stepped out, a bridge instantly appeared out of the invisible realm. It was always there. He just didn't see it.

There are realms of reality that elude us because we do not have the eyes to see them. But the only way to see them is to act. Many say that if they see it they will believe it. But I say that you can only see it if you first believe it. *You don't see it until you begin to walk in it.* Sometimes you have to step out over the edge even though you can't see the bridge that will help you to get to the other side. The power of faith is in the first step. The encouragement to take that step is all around us. There are voices cheering us on, encouraging us to take the leap as they did. The writer of Hebrews knew that well when he wrote: "Therefore we also, since we are surrounded by so great a cloud of witnesses, let us lay aside every weight... and let us run with endurance the race that is set before us, looking unto Jesus, the author and finisher of our faith..." (Heb. 12:1-2, NKJV).

When you lay aside every weight as the Scripture teaches us, you lighten the load of doubt and heighten the level of expectations. Nevertheless, once the load has been lightened, you still have a race to run. You can't decide to hand over your cares and worries to God and then not get in the race. Faith does not eliminate effort. The test of steel is not in its resting but in its stressing. Its strength is not revealed as it sits in the shipping yard. Its might is tested as it is erected and supports the rising structures upon it.

What holds you back? Are you unwilling to make the necessary sacrifices? Do you lack faith? Are you afraid of where the next step will take you? Until you step out in faith, the ideas God has planted in you will never take root and sprout, dreams will never become realities and faith will never become real! Step out in the faith you have NOW!

LIFE PRINCIPLES IN THE CROSSHAIRS:

- **Step out in the faith you have now.**
  As you step out in obedience, your faith will continue to grow. That is one of the dynamic truths about faith. Like our muscles, it grows with exercise. The reverse is also true; it atrophies and becomes stiff with inactivity. As the faith continues to grow, you can then apply it to the situations that are confronting you.

- **Your faith attracts God's blessing.**
  The issue is that the reward follows the faith, not vice versa. If you don't step out in faith, responding to the call of the Lord, then you cannot expect to receive the blessing of the Lord. Father blesses faith, not presumption. Dorothy Parker said, "If you want to know what God thinks of money, just look at the people he gave it to."[4] Abraham was a blessed man but his blessings flowed from his faith and willingness to leave the place of security and go to a place of obscurity.

- **Apply the faith you have right now.**
  As you step out in obedience, your faith will continue to grow. That is one of the dynamic truths about faith. Like

our muscles, it grows with exercise. The reverse is also true; it atrophies and becomes stiff with inactivity. As the faith continues to grow you can then apply it to the situations that are confronting you.

- **If you can't see it, it's not real.**
  We received a call from a church in Toronto that had five buses that they wanted to donate to the ministry. We thought this was great because we couldn't afford to buy any, so we jumped on it. I was 31 years old, just past the stupid stage of life and entering the quasi-moronic stage. However, not all my stupidity was gone. I didn't realize yet that when a church gives something away, it's usually junk. That's why they give it away; if it were any good, they'd keep it for themselves.

- **Are you willing to sacrifice?**
  Money will always be an issue, but you must decide what you want. Are you willing to sacrifice? Is somebody willing to step up to the plate and sacrifice here? It's the story of Zerubbabel all over again (Ezra 4-5). God said to set the foundation of the temple. Zerubbabel said there was no money. However, God said to set the foundation. Just set the foundation! Step out. Get out of the box! Move out!

- **It's time to shut up and step out in faith.**
  Step out. Get out of the box! Move out and do what He told you to do. Oswald Chambers wrote, "Faith is deliberate confidence in the character of God whose ways you may not understand at the time."[5] Your ability to get out of the box is in direct proportion to the understanding you have of the God who has called you to step out.

There will always be critics that say, "Why do you do this? These kids aren't going to last anyway." But I know better. I know that when the fox jumps on the wall of the work, that's a sure sign that it's going to succeed. I've watched so many of these kids and I'm proud of them. I'm proud of what they've done with their lives by the grace of God.

—Bill Wilson

If you are going to have ideas ahead of the times you will have to get used to living with the fact that most people are going to believe you are in the wrong.

—Anonymous

The men who build the future are those who know that greater things are yet to come, and that they themselves will help bring them about. Their minds are illuminated by the blazing sun of hope. They never stop to doubt. They haven't time.

—Melvin J. Evans

CHAPTER 3

AN EFFECT THAT ENDURES

The doubters and detractors criticized Nehemiah by saying that even if a fox climbed on the wall it would collapse (see Neh. 4:3). What were they insinuating with this sarcastic and spiteful remark? This was just another bucket of criticism drawn from the well of their cynical hearts and dumped upon Nehemiah in an attempt to lower him to their feeble positions. In reality, there is no subtlety here. It is very clear what they were suggesting. "It won't last," they said. "It'll fall apart right away. What you are building will not support any sort of pressure whatsoever."

Unfortunately, I've heard these same sad songs during my time in New York. The words are different, but the insidious intents are the same:

> "Why do you even try to change these kids? They're never going to amount to anything. What can you do with those drug addicts whose lives are wasted by their own self-indulgence? They'll just go back to using again. Why do you spend your time with those 11-year-olds that were sold into prostitution by their own mothers? They're not going to amount to anything."

> The most common question people ask is, "What are those kids going to become?"

It's a question expressing skepticism in the future success of these kids, my kids. "Certainly," they think, "these kids cannot become doctors or lawyers. They will never emerge as productive contributors in our society." I fight back and tell them, "You're right. They're probably not going to become doctors and lawyers in your small world. But they will get jobs and raise families."

For instance, a good job in my neighborhood is a garbage collector. They make $30,000 a year. In fact, I was just thinking about doing it myself. It's not a bad deal. You see success is a matter of your cultural perspective. Maybe in your world becoming a doctor or lawyer is a sign of success. In my world, getting free from drugs, getting a job and raising a family is a sign of greater success.

On the other hand, if you prefer, they can become a lookout working for the local drug dealers. Hey, these kids can make good money in this business. Twelve-year-old kids make $100 a day in cash. All they have to do is whistle when they see the cops. There are some kids making $700 a week, cash. It's easy for the casual observer to stand on the outside and criticize and take a cynical position. But you have no idea the challenges these kids face. It's hard to get motivated to work in a fast-food restaurant at minimum wage when you can make $700 a week whistling for the drug dealers.

So, the question you ask me is what these kids will become. I'm not nearly as interested in *what* these kids become, as in what they *don't* become. No, they're not all going to be model citizens, but we can help them survive in this urban jungle. Another thing, they will never become what they were destined unless somebody intervenes. That's the difference. You can either stand on the outside the circle and take a suspicious position, or you can get inside the circle and try to make a difference. It's easy to *criticize* what others are doing but, believe me, it is more rewarding to *change* what others are doing. Theodore Roosevelt put it best this way at his speech in Paris, 1910:

> It is not the critic who counts, not the man who points out how the strong man stumbled, or where the doer of deeds could have done better. The credit belongs to the man who is actually in the arena, whose face is marred by dust and sweat and blood, who strives valiantly, who errs and comes short again and again, who knows the great enthusiasms, the great devotions, and spends himself in a worthy cause, who at best knows achievement and who at the worst if he fails at least fails while daring greatly so that his place shall never be with those cold and timid souls who know neither victory nor defeat.[1]

THE PROMISE OF DESTINY

Most people don't understand that destiny carries with it a promise. As you move toward your destiny, the promise of that destiny kicks in and moves you faster along the road to fulfillment.

Destiny is powerful, gripping the heart and soul with such force that it's nearly impossible to get free. William Jennings Bryan said that destiny is not a matter of chance, it is a matter of choice; it is not a thing to be waited for, it is a thing to be achieved.[2] When you begin to make the right choices, a power within develops that will propel you to the promise of your destiny.

The promise of your destiny is the glue that keeps you intact and on the track to its fulfillment. No matter what the nature of your destiny might be, its promise remains, always standing before you. You may seek to elude it in the pursuit of other things, but the hands of promise are always reaching out to you, seeking to draw you into its arms.

I can't tell you how many kids I've seen raised in these drug-infested streets. Their mentality is much different than the ones looking in from the outside. These kids see a *career* with great reward, while an outsider sees the *crime* that should be punished. It all depends on your perspective, on what side of the river you are standing. If you don't think that there will be any other choice in life, then you will hop on the first train that goes by and hope it takes you somewhere decent. I've seen kids who've been raised so long in such poverty that they have become accustomed to it. They don't know they could have it any other way. They don't know that any other world exists. They have lived their whole lives in a flat world of crime and poverty.

Unless you've been there and unless you have experienced the despair of not having anywhere to turn, you can't appreciate the mind-set that is formed in these circumstances. It's easy when you've been raised in an environment of encouragement and been told to expand your horizons and given opportunity to see the world. But it's nearly impossible to dream of another life when you live in filth every day and are just trying to get through the next day without starving or getting shot.

I've been there. I've lived it. I know what I'm talking about, because I've been hungry for days, wondering where my next meal was coming from. I've lived from place to place, not able to call any one of them my home. I've been left to take care of myself when I didn't know how or where to start. I guess that is one of the reasons I am so in love with and passionate about these kids.

Because of my life, I know that there is hope for theirs. I found my destiny, and it is my life to help others make their own discoveries.

We're here to create a different destiny, paint a different picture of the future for these kids. We're here to let them know that there is a promise and a future that doesn't include drugs or poverty. We're here to let them know that God loves them and wants the best for them.

TO PLANT IS TO HOPE

What farmer plants his field with no hope of a harvest? What investor puts his money into an account with no hope of a return? What kind of God would put His creatures on a planet with no hope of a future?

I'm like a farmer or an investor. I see the field and the potential in it. Farmers don't look at a field and see it barren and unplowed. They look at a field and see the harvest. Well, God is the same way. When He looks at us, He sees a harvest. "'For I know the plans I have for you,' declares the Lord, 'plans to prosper you and not to harm you, plans to give you hope and a future'" (Jer. 29:11, NIV).

Have you ever looked at a kid and been able to discern his future? Maybe it's time you did. Maybe it's time you stopped thinking about your own stuff and started thinking about someone else. Maybe it's time to see the future in another person and help turn it away from the destructive course it is on.

No man is an island. Your destiny is always overlapped with the destiny of others. On your journey to fulfill your dreams, you will be assisting others to find their destiny. The joy of the journey is when you are able to turn a light on in someone else's life, helping them to see the possibility of a promising future.

Every time I look into the eyes of one of my kids, hope is kindled in my heart. I don't see what others see. I have a different set of eyes. I see possibilities, not problems. If it were not this way, I would have checked out a long time ago. I know what it's like to have someone stop, pay attention to me, and give me a minute of his time. After my mom abandoned me, I sat by the road for three days wondering what to do next. Finally, a man who'd seen me in the same place during those days decided to stop. He must have caught a glimmer of hope in me, because he gave me a place to stay. He set me on a path that eventually led me to New York City and Metro. There is nothing like someone making a sacrifice to kindle a flame in your life. Henry Ward Beecher got it right when he said, "A helping word to one in trouble is often like a switch on a railroad track… an inch between wreck and smooth, rolling prosperity."[3] We will never know the power of an encouraging word spoken into the life of one in whom the light of hope has been snuffed out.

Don't be afraid to take a risk. You never know how the kid you have reached out to with a helping hand might grow up to be because of your investment in his life. Sure, it's tough going sometimes. All good deeds have a price tag attached to them. Anything worth doing will cost you something, but I can assure you that whatever the price, saving a life is worth it.

By the way, don't expect to be cheered on by others when you are trying to make a difference. Like Nehemiah, you will have to listen to those losers around you telling you that it's a waste of time. Those who will make a difference in the lives of others are those who have learned to shut their ears to those hecklers standing on the sidelines. Notice that they are more content to criticize others' actions as opposed to getting involved in the game themselves. These armchair quarterbacks are worthless when it comes to creating success on the field of life.

Good Seed Sown Into Good Soil Produces Good Fruit

Will it last? I'm not going to stand up here and tell you that every kid we win grows up to be a model citizen. However, I've discovered that one out of four do. It's not much different than the parable of the sower whose seed fell into the four kinds of soil (see Matt. 13:1-9). Over the years I have noticed that this is just about how our work has averaged out. Some of the seed falls on good soil, some of it doesn't. But we can never be the premature judges of which ground is the good ground. All you can do is cast your seed on *all* ground and then trust Father for the results. I've been working in the harvest long enough to see that when the seed does fall on good soil and takes root, some pretty amazing things happen. I will never cease to stand in wonder at the glory of a life that has been changed because someone took the time to plant a little seed.

The kids that were riding the buses 15 years ago are now driving those buses and many of them are now part of our staff.

They're growing up, getting married, and raising their own kids in the knowledge of Christ. Many of them have gone to Bible school. I rejoice in the reality of what so many people have said that they never could become.

Has it been easy? Nope. It's been a very long, arduous road. It's been very hard and very difficult for all of us, for the kids as well as every one of us that has chosen to work with them. I've not always see the instant result I've hoped for. I've experienced disappointments, faced repeated financial challenges, and paid a great price physically for this ministry. But in the end, I have great joy as I have watched countless lives being changed by the love of Jesus as expressed through my fellow co-workers and me. Yes, it has been worth it all.

WHAT ABOUT THE FOXES?

Sometimes people do their very best to make themselves look more negative and stupid than anyone else. The stones of the wall built by Nehemiah's workers were huge! They were designed to be walked on and to withstand any aggressive attack from the enemies of Israel. They were placed together in such a way that each stone locked the ones next to it. This was not shabby construction done by careless contractors.

How foolish it must have sounded to Nehemiah and the others building the wall to suggest that a fox could bring it down by simply jumping on it. At times, you just need to put the comments into context and consider the source. Some people will think of the most brainless thing to say in an effort to try to create doubt and drag you down to their miserable level of life. Don't go there!

I've been bombarded over the years by some off-the-wall things. They bothered me at first until, after a while, I noticed that they all began to sound the same. It's crazy, but it's almost like the same voice was speaking all the time. The more I heard it, the easier it was to recognize. Then it hit me. It was the same voice. All the negative, nasty, naysaying nonsense springs from the same source—the well of bitter water created by the evil one who has come and polluted the waters.

Here's what I've learned. Because it's coming from the same source, it's the same enemy. Instead of fighting a multitude, I'm fighting only one. Because I'm fighting only one, I can take hold of the promise in the Scriptures that says that one will put an army of a thousand to flight:

> *How could one chase a thousand, and two put ten thousand to flight, unless their Rock had sold them, and the Lord had surrendered them? For their rock is not like our Rock...* (Deut. 32:30-31a, NKJV).

Someone is always there, waiting in the wings to steal your enthusiasm and make your task more difficult. Usually they are the ones who don't have the energy, willingness, desire, or vision to do what you're doing. They would be happier if you were just as lazy as they are. To be truthful, it is your consistent commitment to Father's work that creates such pangs of jealousy and shame in their life. They have only two choices. They can change their attitude and join you. Or, they must cover their shame and jealousy by attempting to expose your weaknesses and seeking to bring you back down to their pitiful plane.

Don't fall into the trap of letting others compare you to themselves. Comparisons with others will only lead you down the path of discouragement. Instead, allow yourself to be covered by the grace and greatness of the One that you serve. Flee the presence of these doomsayers and pursue the presence of the One that can give you strength for the task He has assigned to you.

GO AHEAD—JUMP ON IT!

Nehemiah wasn't concerned with the words of these negative, stinkin' thinkin' people. He'd heard from God and that was enough. This is a great key for all those who would seek to serve the purposes of God in this generation. Give attention to the voice of God and quickly obey His words. What you hear in the private place, prepare yourself to bring to pass in the public place! What you have heard in the secret places of God will strengthen you against those who would oppose you.

What are you going to do when others criticize your work? What are you going to say when people try to shoot you down by telling you that what you're doing won't last? Are you going to listen to them and give up or are you going to listen to God and keep building?

Time after time, I would challenge those who criticized me to just dig in and do it themselves. "C'mon, stand by me and let's work together to build this thing." The problem was clear. They weren't interested in building. They were only interested in tearing down. What are you interested in?

The challenge is yours today. Are you going to let the nagging naysayers have their way? Why not challenge them, asking them to climb right up on the wall and jump up and down and see if they can bring it down? Tell them to pick up a stone to place it in the appropriate place as opposed to throwing it at others. Better to position stones into God's work than to throw stones at God's workers. Your response to them will speak volumes. They may not hear it, but others who are watching you will. Those who appreciate the vision, dedication, and work you've given to God will become a blessing in your life.

Go ahead. Jump on it! Test it. Try it. Show them that it will stand. No voice of criticism should shut down your God-given vision. Be open to hear God's voice of encouragement. It will empower you to complete the job, even when you're tired.

C'mon, let's get up on that wall and do a few jumping jacks!

LIFE PRINCIPLES IN THE CROSSHAIRS:

- **Build what will endure.**
  The naysayers criticized Nehemiah by saying that even if a fox climbed on the wall it would collapse. This was just more of the same criticism that was heaped upon Nehemiah by negative, shortsighted people. "It won't last," they said. "It'll fall apart right away." I've heard a lot of this same stuff in New York:
  "So the question you ask me is what these kids will become. I'm not nearly as interested in *what* these kids become, as in what they *don't* become. No, they're not all going to be model citizens, but you know what? We can help them survive in this urban jungle." Another thing, they will never become what they were destined unless somebody intervenes. That's the difference. You can either stand outside the circle and take a suspicious position, or you can get inside the circle and try to make a difference.

- **The promise of destiny.**
  Most people don't understand that destiny carries with it a promise. As you move toward your destiny, the

promise of that destiny kicks in and moves you faster along the road to fulfillment. Destiny is powerful, gripping the heart and soul with such force that it's nearly impossible to get free. When you begin to make the right choices, a power within develops that will propel you to the promise of your destiny.

The promise of your destiny is the glue that keeps you intact and on the track to its fulfillment. No matter what the nature of your destiny might be, its promise is always standing before you. You may seek to elude it in the pursuit of other things, but the hands of promise are always reaching out to you, seeking to draw you into its arms.

- **To plant is to hope.**
  Every time I look into the eyes of one of my kids, hope is kindled in my heart. I don't see what others see. I have a different set of eyes. I see possibilities, not problems. If it were not this way, I would have checked out a long time ago. I know what it's like to have someone stop, pay attention to me, and give me a minute of his time. After my mom abandoned me, I sat by the road for three days, wondering what to do next. Finally, a man who'd seen me in the same place during those days decided to stop. He must have caught a glimmer of hope in me, because he gave me a place to stay. He set me on a path that eventually led me to New York City and Metro. There is nothing like someone making a sacrifice to kindle a flame in your life.

- **Good seed sown into good soil produces good fruit.**
  Will it last? I'm not going to stand up here and tell you that every kid we win grows up to be a model citizen. However, I've discovered that one out of four do. It's not much different than the parable of the sower whose seed fell into the four kinds of soil (Matt 13:1-9). Over the years I have noticed that this is just about how our work has averaged out. Some of the seed falls on good soil, some of it doesn't. But we should never judge prematurely which ground is the good ground. All you can do

is cast your seed on *all* ground and then trust Father for the results.

- **What about the foxes?**
  Someone is always there, waiting in the wings to steal your enthusiasm and make your task more difficult. Usually they are the ones who don't have the energy, willingness, desire, or vision to do what you're doing. They would be happier if you were just as lazy as they are. To be truthful, it is your consistent commitment to Father's work that creates such pangs of jealousy and shame in their lives. They have only two choices. They can change their attitude and join you. Or, they must cover their shame and jealousy by attempting to expose your weaknesses, seeking to bring you back down to their pitiful plane.

- **Go ahead—jump on it!**
  The challenge is yours today. Are you going to let the nagging naysayers have their way? Why not challenge them, asking them to climb right up on the wall and jump up and down and see if they can bring it down? Tell them to pick up a stone to place it in the appropriate place, as opposed to throwing it at others. Better to position stones into God's work than throw stones at God's workers. Your response to them will speak volumes.

The devil doesn't want you to know your destiny. He knows that if you discover your destiny, he's history; it's that simple. If the devil can keep you away, or if he can keep you blinded and surrounded by people that constantly question you and talk down to you, then he knows that you'll never be what you're supposed to be.

—Bill Wilson

The future belongs to those who believe in the beauty of their dreams.

—Eleanor Roosevelt

I cannot change yesterday I can only make the most of today, and look with hope towards tomorrow.

—Anonymous

I don't know what your destiny will be, but one thing I do know: The only ones among you who will be really happy are those who have sought and found how to serve.

—Albert Schweitzer

CHAPTER **4**

A MIND THAT MATTERED

But it so happened, when Sanballat heard that we were re-building the wall, that he was furious and very indignant, and mocked the Jews. And he spoke before his brethren and the army of Samaria, and said, "What are these feeble Jews doing…Will they complete it in a day?" (Neh. 4:1-2, NKJV)

Negative, stinkin' thinkin' people all sound the same. "Nehemiah, can you finish the wall in one day?" It's interesting, isn't it? Here's the cheering squad again, sowing seeds of doubt and negativity. It's a good thing that Nehemiah listened to God instead of that cheerful bunch gathered around to watch him fail. It took him and his work crew fifty-two days to complete the job, no thanks to this despicable lot.

Some people get enjoyment out of dropping little seeds of doubt and discouragement into your life, in an attempt to get you to start questioning yourself. Whatever you do, don't take the bait. Don't get on their bandwagon—it's going nowhere. Those who have accomplished much in life have learned how to turn a deaf ear to their critics. It is an irreversible rule of life. He who attempts to accomplish great things will always be swatting at the irritating gnats of criticism swarming around his efforts. But that is all they are—irritating gnats—that offer no true resistance to those who are committed to the task.

Martin Luther King, Jr., who faced quite a few pesky gnats in his lifetime, said, "The ultimate measure of a man is not where he stands in moments of comfort and convenience, but where he stands at times of challenge and controversy."[1] It is inevitable that you will face opposition. The key to your success is how you handle that opposition.

THE YOUNG, THE BRAVE, THE CRAZY

In remembering the days when I first went to New York, I now realize I may have been nuts. It was truly the blind leading the blind. Consider this:

- I was young and crazy enough, and maybe inexperienced enough to really think I could do it.

- I went by myself with no background and no support.

- I got my own apartment (well, sort of) in the middle of a dangerous city.

- I paid drug dealers to drive the buses and got non-Christian kids to invite other kids.

When I first arrived, I rode the subway to get a feel for the city. Once, while I was riding the train, some guy came and sat next to me who:

- smelled funny

- looked like he had horns on his head

- had something that looked like a pointed tail sticking out of the back of his pants

- smelled like smoke.

He leaned over and said, "I hear you're starting a Sunday school."

I said, "Yeah, hot dog! Boy, I'm excited. I can't wait. We're going to do it!"

He replied, "Yeah, how many kids you got in that Sunday school?"

I proudly responded, "Well, I don't have any yet, but we're going to, we're going to."

We rode a couple more stops and then he said again, "I hear you're starting a Sunday school."

I said, "Yeah, hot dog, it's going to be great! I can't wait!"

He then questioned me, "Who's going to pay for this, how much money you got?"

I said, "Well, I don't have any money right now. But, we're going to have some soon, I know we are."

We rode a few more stops and I heard his words one more time, "I hear you're going to start a Sunday school."

"Yeah," I said. "Hot dog, I can hardly wait now."

Deviously, he asked, "How much staff do you have?"

"Don't have any," I responded.

Again, he questioned me, "Who's going to do all this?"

Once more I replied, "I don't know."

We went one more stop, and he said again, "I hear you're starting a Sunday school."

"Yeah," I said.

At the next stop, do you know what I did? When the doors opened, I picked him up and threw him off the train! The devil comes in all shapes and sizes, folks. The devil will come during times of your heaviest battle and greatest challenge. It's then that you must plow forward with the faith that you have and step out and do what you know God has told you to do.

It is quite clear that the devil doesn't want you to know your destiny. He knows that if you discover your destiny, he's history. It's that simple. If the devil can keep you away from your field of dreams, or if he can keep you blinded and surrounded by people that constantly question you and talk down to you, then he knows that you'll never be what you're supposed to be. It is critical to your success that you know how to effectively withstand such verbal abuse from the enemy.

PICK YOUR ASSOCIATES CAREFULLY

I'm extremely careful about the kind of people I spend time around. I don't need to spend time around negative people, and neither do you. Pessimists are blind to the possibilities that are all around us. Churchill certainly faced a number of these Sad Sacks who lacked any kind of vision. "A pessimist sees the difficulty in every opportunity; an optimist sees the opportunity in every difficulty."[2] I want to surround myself with people who have vision for the possible and not those who are blind to opportunity.

We have seen the damage that negativism can do. You've seen it in the church and you've seen it in your own life. Don't go there. One of the worst things you can do is surround yourself with people who don't think you will amount to anything. Do you honestly think you'll get any encouragement from them? Concerning this gloomy group of downbeats, Helen Keller wrote, "No pessimist ever discovered the secret of the stars, or sailed to an uncharted land, or opened a new doorway for the human spirit."[3]

Choose not to sit around negative people. You've seen them. It's like the "going out to eat after church crowd." They disguise it by calling it fellowship, but usually when they get together, they get billy-goat religion. You know, "Pastor's a nice guy but..." then they'll "but" him around for awhile. "Well, that's a good word, but...." Don't surround yourself with such diseased people who have no vision for the future! King David put it this way, "How blessed is the man who does not walk in the counsel of the wicked, nor stand in the path of sinners, Nor sit in the seat of scoffers!"[4]

If you hang around enough drug dealers, you'll begin to act like them and pretty soon, you'll be like them. If you hang with a crowd that's negative and sour on life, you'll become negative and sour on life as well. However, if you mix with a crowd that's positive and excited to do the work of God, guess what? You'll become more positive and will get excited about working for the Lord. Find people who will lift you up rather than drag you down, broaden your horizons rather than constrict them. Pursue those who will challenge you to attempt great things, rather than censure you for your attempts at the impossible.

HAVE A POSITIVE MIND-SET

Nehemiah forcefully declared that he was not coming down from the wall until the work was done. He had a mind-set that was committed to the task at hand and would not be distracted by negativity. I like that—he had a determined mind-set to work. I love driving the bus in New York— narrow streets, lots of people, and nobody cares. I love it. That is my attitude about my work—positive, encouraging to others, and refreshing to me. Driving the bus is just an extension of my life. I like sharing with others what I've learned in New York and in starting sidewalk Sunday schools in other countries. I enjoy mixing it up with people and getting involved with their problems, helping them find answers to their issues. I enjoy the challenge of the chase, of getting right out in the middle of the work.

I like to be on the front lines and don't understand why people want to hang out in the back. I like being up front because, if something happens, I want to stick my nose right in it. If somebody's going to get in a fight, I want to take the first swing. That's just the way I am. I love being in the middle of what is happening. I don't like the atmosphere at the back of the crowd.

Nehemiah had a positive mind-set to work hard and accomplish what God had commissioned him to do. He couldn't complete the job in a day or a week, but by positively facing each day and pushing through each little task, he finally finished the job.

Search Out Others Willing to Work

Nehemiah didn't rebuild the wall by himself. Other people were around to help him make the bricks, mix the mortar, lay the bricks, and stand guard with swords. You need others! The support staff—the people watching over the work as well as the people backing you up—are all necessary. You need people who will stand alongside you with the same vision to complete the work. If you think you can do it alone, you're setting yourself up for failure. Don't be afraid to seek out others who are willing to work with you.

Teamwork is the fuel that allows common people to attain uncommon results. More can be done by the power of a unified group than the strength of any single great person. When Thomas Edison was asked why he had a team of twenty-one assistants, he responded by saying that if he could solve all the problems himself, he would.

The story of Nehemiah's support staff needs to be implemented in modern day Christianity. I wish today that we had a combination of both. Sadly, that's often not the case. Today, many Christians only want to be the head guy, the whole enchilada, and the only hotdog.

We don't need any more hotdogs. We need people who are willing to step up and simply be a contributing member of the team. If it means mixing concrete, changing a bus engine, knocking on doors, or whatever, we need people that will tackle the job without caring who gets the credit or even if nobody ever sees what they did.

That's what you need to do. If it means being a part of a support staff, then do it. That's a decision you must make in your own life. Here's a principle of God that needs to sink deep inside your soul: God promotes from within. He moves you up through the ranks, not over them. So, start where you are today and see how God begins to move you.

DETERMINE WITHIN YOURSELF THAT YOU WILL FINISH!

Not long ago, the knuckles on my right hand began to cause me a lot of pain. Because I knew I was getting older, I thought it was arthritis starting to creep in. I went to the doctor to have it examined and he decided to do an X-ray. After the doctor was done with all the tests, he asked what I had done to damage my hand. When he showed me the X-rays, I saw that on two of the knuckles there were numerous hairline cracks. The doctor asked if I had ever been in a car wreck or had damaged my hand somehow. I told him that I've totaled nine rental cars, so he asked if I remembered smashing my hand in one. When I told him no, he asked if I had ever been in a plane crash. I told him that I'd been in three plane crashes. Again, he asked if I remembered smashing my hand and again I said, "No." Finally, it occurred to me. For thirty years, I've been knocking on doors. As a result, two knuckles on my right hand are shattered. The doctor told me I couldn't do that anymore, but I said, "Yeah, I can, and when these go, I'll use my left hand. When they go out, I'll just kick the stupid thing."

Why? Because I have a vision and I am determined to make that vision a reality. You can allow yourself to become *discouraged*, or you can remain *determined* in your efforts to finish your mission. We have a song that we sing called, *"Whose report will you believe?"* I don't know about you, but I'm going to believe the report of the Lord.

I believe the report of the Lord, and my faith in Him has inspired and encouraged me to move forward. I'll go out kicking and screaming if I have to. Like I told the doctor, if I can't use my right hand, then I'll use my left. If I can't do that, then I'll kick the door. That's what Nehemiah did; he said he was not coming down until the job was done.

"Oh no! You can't do that!"

"Oh no! It costs too much money!"

"Oh no! It's not going to last!"

"Oh no!"

There they are again—the voices from the land of ONO. It doesn't change, does it? Not in organized religion, and unfortunately, not among your friends and not in your family.

Nothing ever changes. We continue to face the exact same stuff Nehemiah fought. Nevertheless, he kept at it until the task was done.

A Masterchief of the Navy Seals described what it took to survive their training with these words:

It takes a little courage,
And a little self-control.
And some grim determination,
If you want to reach the goal.

It takes a great deal of striving,
And a firm and stern-set chin.
No matter what the battle,
If you really want to win.

There's no easy path to glory.
There is no road to fame.
Life, however we may view it,
Is no simple parlor game.

But its prizes call for fighting,
For endurance and for grit,
For a rugged disposition,
That will not quit.[5]

No matter what the battle, if you really want to win, there's no easy path to glory. This is the truth that all must hear if they choose to successfully complete any task in life.

IF IT'S WORTHWHILE, IT TAKES TIME TO BUILD

When the world says it will take too long, do you believe them? When someone becomes a Christian, do you think he should be perfect right from the start? Well, I've got news for you: They're not going to be perfect; they'll make mistakes. They will not be Mr. or Mrs. Perfect Christian overnight. The Christian life is a journey that is not completed in one day, one week, or one year. It takes a lifetime, and because I understand this basic truth, I have been able to overcome discouragement when there seems to be setbacks in the lives of some of these kids.

No matter what we build or what we're dealing with, it takes time. Sadly, many in our day are living with a fast-food mentality.

We like it quick and cheap. We like "drive-thru" ministry—I'll tell you what I want, I'll pay you and when I get it, I am out of here. We just want life our way. If we can't have it our way, we don't want it even though our way might not be the best way.

Negative people never have the energy to take the time or exert the effort to finish what they're building. So, walk away from negative associates. Surround yourself with positive, supportive people to help you build the vision God has given you. Then watch as the work rises daily before your very eyes. Watch as the ministry grows and the job gets done in God's timing. If your dream has any value, believe me, it will take time to reach your goal. Patience is not a defining characteristic of today's culture, but it is the defining characteristic of all the lives of those who have ever accomplished any great thing.

Because I believe in God, I believe in you. If God has given you a task, then He trusts you. Decide today that you will take the time and exert the effort needed to complete the charge placed before you.

LIFE PRINCIPLES IN THE CROSSHAIRS:

- **Don't listen to negative people.**
  Negative, stinkin' thinkin' people all sound the same. Some people get enjoyment out of dropping little seeds of doubt and discouragement into your life to try to get you to start questioning yourself. Whatever you do, don't take the bait. Don't get on their bandwagon; it's going nowhere.

- **The young, the brave, the crazy.**
  It is quite clear that the devil doesn't want you to know your destiny. He knows that if you discover your destiny, he's history. It's that simple. If the devil can keep you away from your field of dreams, or if he can keep you blinded and surrounded by people that constantly question you and talk down to you, then he knows that you'll never be what you're supposed to be. It is critical to your success that you know how to effectively withstand such verbal abuse from the enemy.

- **Pick your associates carefully.**
  I'm extremely careful about the kind of people I spend time around. I don't need to spend time around negative

people, and neither do you. Pessimists are blind to the possibilities that are all around us. Churchill certainly faced a number of these Sad Sacks who lacked any kind of vision. "A pessimist sees the difficulty in every opportunity; an optimist sees the opportunity in every difficulty."[6] I want to surround myself with people who have vision for the possible and not those who are blind to opportunity.

- **Have a positive mind-set.**
  Nehemiah had a positive mind-set to work hard and accomplish what God had commissioned him to do. He couldn't complete the job in a day or a week, but by positively facing each day and pushing through each little task, he finally finished the job.

- **Search out others willing to work.**
  You need others! The support staff—the people watching over the work as well as the people backing you up—are all necessary to the completion of the task at hand. You need people who will stand alongside you with the same vision to complete the work. If you think you can do it alone, you're setting yourself up for failure. Don't be afraid to seek out others who are willing to work with you.

- **Determine within yourself that you will finish!**
  I believe the report of the Lord, and my faith in Him has inspired and encouraged me to move forward. I'll go out kicking and screaming if I have to. Like I told the doctor, if I can't use my right hand, then I'll use my left. If I can't do that, then I'll kick the door. That's what Nehemiah did; he said he was not coming down until the job was done.

- **If it's worthwhile, it takes time to build.**
  When the world says it will take too long, do you believe them? When someone becomes a Christian, do you think he should be perfect right from the start?
  If your dream has any value, believe me, it will take time to reach your goal. Patience is not a defining characteristic of today's culture, but it is the defining characteristic of all the lives of those who have ever accomplished any great thing.

Once you've been in the battle, and you've seen the wall start to go up—once you've seen some enemies defeated—it does something to you. You feel in complete cooperation with God. But when you step down—the minute you come off that wall and entertain quitting—you're opening yourself up to the fact that you may never go back up. I don't know about you, but I'm not taking that risk.

—Bill Wilson

Most people give up just when they're about to achieve success. They quit on the one yard line. They give up at the last minute of the game, one foot from a winning touchdown.

—H. Ross Perot

What this power is, I cannot say. All I know is that it exists...and it becomes available only when you are in that state of mind in which you know EXACTLY what you want...and are fully determined not to quit until you get it.

—Alexander Graham Bell

CHAPTER 5

A Resistance That Revives

He spoke in the presence of his brothers and the wealthy men of Samaria and said, "What are these feeble Jews doing? Are they going to restore it for themselves? Can they offer sacrifices? Can they finish in a day? Can they revive the stones from the dusty rubble even the burned ones?" Now Tobiah the Ammonite was near him and he said, "Even what they are building—if a fox should jump on it, he would break their stone wall down!" (Neh. 4:2-3, NASB)

The city of Jerusalem had been devastated by marauding bands of thugs. The defensive walls of the city had been torn down and left in piles of rubble. One of Nehemiah's first tasks was to rebuild these walls, creating a perimeter of protection for the city. Imagine this critical crowd, crowing their disparaging words at Nehemiah. "Hey! Nehemiah, do you actually think that something can live again? Do you think you can take the rubble and make something out of it?"

Can something actually be brought back after being devastated? That is a very relevant question. These self-righteous critics were quick to cast their stones of verbal abuse. It was easy for them to stand on the sidelines, making their snide remarks. It doesn't cost a thing to sit and criticize. Their doubt would be their doom, because God intended to restore the things that had been devastated.

Some of the lives we have touched in New York were on the brink of destruction. Many of these young lives have seen everything by the time they are 11 years old. They've seen it all, and they've been through it all. They have lived in a world of rejection, drugs, violence, abuse, and great pain. Every day I am amazed at the lives that have been changed. Most of us would have betted against these kids' chances for survival. Kids like:

- The little boy that couldn't talk because of the terrible, abusive acts committed against him. He would just play with a toy car while one of our teachers sat with him, telling him that we loved him.

- A young boy who was crying uncontrollably during one Mother's Day weekend. His mom had told him the day before that she didn't want him and was sending him away. He said, "I bought her a Mother's Day present, but she still doesn't want me."

- A boy bought his absentee father a birthday card. When he finally tracked him down in the Bronx and gave him the card, the father ripped it up and sent it back.

Often, when I reach out to just touch them and tousle their hair or tweak their little noses, they duck their heads or put their heads down and turn away. Why? Because all they've ever known are adults swinging their hands out to hit them.

CAN THESE STONES COME TO LIFE?

People often ask me if I really think I can make a difference in the lives of these kids. A few don't turn out right and some don't stick with it, so when the critics see that, they are the first to say, "We told you. You poured your guts into that one and now look, it didn't do any good." The critics will always come around to tell you that you're wasting your time. You'll seem to be surrounded by people from the land of ONO. They'll shout at you, saying, "Oh no":

- "Nothing good has ever come out of that rat hole."

- "Your parents didn't make it; why do you think you're going to make it?"

- "They used to live for God and now they're not doing so good. I told you. I told you they couldn't do it. Why did you even think they could be Christians?"

- "You can't make a difference in this city; nobody's ever done it before, so who are you?"

- "What qualifies you when nobody else has been able to do it?"

Nehemiah faced a decision. He knew that something needed to be done and nobody else was doing it. We don't know if he knew the criticism would come, but he was smart enough to know how to handle it when it did.

When Nehemiah was faced with this pessimistic pounding by these cynical couch potatoes, he had to decide what to do. He knew that once he came off the wall, even if it was only once, the race would be over. He also knew that he couldn't get involved in a defensive dialogue with the crowd that was trying to divert his attention. Therefore, he decided to ignore them. Just don't talk with the crowd of critics! Let them drown in their sea of skepticism. I have work to do.

ATTEMPT GREAT THINGS, ACCOMPLISH GREAT THINGS

I've survived in New York City because I've learned to ignore people's "advice." When someone tells me to step down and take a rest, I don't do it. Several have taken me to task on this, but I know that if I will just continue to stay on the wall, God somehow will fight the battle for me. Quitting is not an option. Even the most ordinary person can accomplish great things if they refuse give up. George Allen, the great football coach, put it this way: "People of mediocre ability sometimes achieve outstanding success because they don't know when to quit. Most men succeed because they are determined to."[1]

Once you've been in the battle and you've seen the wall start to go up—once you've seen some enemies defeated—something happens to you. You feel like you are completely cooperating with God. However, when you step down—the minute you come off that wall and entertain quitting—you open yourself up to the possibility that you may never go back. There is the danger of losing the energy and the vision that has inspired you in the midst of the greatest battles. I don't know about you, but I'm not taking that risk.

Why do you think I didn't quit when I had tuberculosis? Many people think I've got a martyr complex, but I don't. I just knew that if I went down, I might not go back up. It was the most critical time of year and during the most important time of fund-raising—we were preparing for Christmas. I am a bit stubborn, but it is because I am driven by the vision that God has given me and if I don't finish this task, who will?

Some have asked if God spoke to me. He didn't have to. I already had a word from God. It is found in the words of Jesus when He said that to love Him means feeding the sheep.

> *So when they had eaten breakfast, Jesus said to Simon Peter, "Simon, son of Jonah, do you love Me more than these?" He said to Him, "Yes, Lord; You know that I love You." He said to him, "Feed My lambs." He said to him again a second time, "Simon, son of Jonah, do you love Me?" He said to Him, "Yes, Lord; You know that I love You." He said to him, "Tend My sheep." He said to him the third time, "Simon, son of Jonah, do you love Me?" Peter was grieved because He said to him the third time, "Do you love Me?" And he said to Him, "Lord, You know all things; You know that I love You." Jesus said to him, "Feed My sheep" (John 21:15-17, NKJV).*

Jesus made it clear that your love for Him is manifested in how you take care of those sheep in His world. The power of His love should be a driving force in our lives, leading us into constant encounters with those who are broken and hurting in this world.

It is easy to get wrapped up in ritualistic performance of our religious duties and yet miss the little opportunities all around us. Do you really love Him? If so, you'll love what He loves. Jesus said, "For God so loved the world that He gave His only begotten Son" (John 3:16a, NKJV). Why? Love. See, when the Lord is in the battle, it's because of love. And you can stay in the battle because of love. Love empowers you to overcome your own self-will and submit to the One who is all-loving. Once you have stepped into that kind of love, there is no way that you can abandon those who are longing for just a little bit of love.

DON'T QUIT

The temptation to quit is always strongest when the battle is raging hot and heavy, but what usually marks a winner is his determination to not quit. Leonardo da Vinci, scientist, inventor, and artist, described determination with these words: "Obstacles cannot crush me. Every obstacle yields to stern resolve. He who is fixed to a star does not change his mind."[2]

I've never quit and I'm not going to. I say that publicly to keep myself accountable. So now I'm stuck. I've had people say, "If

Bill Wilson can keep on going with as much
then so can I." They're right! If I can do it, ꜰ
    Nehemiah had to make a choice and i
of constant criticism, inadequate finances, ꞈ
sources he kept working to reach his goal. Sounds famꞈ
it? Have you ever started a project with less than you needeꞈ.
    Nehemiah battled the same things that you and I do in every
day of our lives. It doesn't matter whether it's family, ministry, or a
job. You can either get discouraged, or you can become determined—
it's your call. Voices from the land of ONO will always surround
you, trying to bring you down. So, the next time somebody comes
up to you and says, "*Oh no!*" you can say, "Oh yeah! I can do that.
Because I can do all things."

ONE CAN MAKE A DIFFERENCE
    Lower Australia has a beach that's about two miles long.
Several times a year, thousands of starfish are washed up on the
beach in high tide. Most of them are washed back out to sea when
the tide goes back out, but occasionally they remain on the beach.
If they lie in the sun for any length of time, the starfish dry up
and die.
    Once, a tourist was jogging down the beach at dawn. As he
ran, he could see thousands of starfish on the beach and in the distance, a young person throwing something into the sea. As he was
watching, it looked as if the person was throwing stones to skip
them on the water. However, as the tourist came closer, he saw that
a young man was picking up starfish and throwing them back out
into the surf.
    The tourist went up to the youth and said, "I know what
you're doing and why you're doing it, but there are a couple of
miles of beach and thousands of starfish. Do you really think this
will make a difference?" The young man looked at him, picked up
another starfish and threw it into the surf. "I don't know," he said.
"But, it's going to make a difference to that one."

YOU CAN MAKE A DIFFERENCE
    Don't let people discourage you and don't let them question
your call, because they will. When you step out of the box and
choose to be different, you'll see that "different" doesn't fly in "polite" society. Down through the ages, there have been men and

men who defied the odds and went against the stream to accomplish great things.

One of the great lights of social reform in the chronicles of history was the British statesman William Wilberforce. Wilberforce was the key political leader in the abolition of the slave trade. He was a tiny "shrimp" of a man, but he was gigantic in his courage, and tenacious in his struggle against a very popular trade. It was a cause that he believed in and to which he dedicated all of his adult life.

William was strongly influenced in his early life by his aunt and uncle, who were very much involved in Methodism. He would later declare to his mother that George Whitefield had put something of a fire in his heart that would remain forever. The Methodist had taught him the importance of getting involved in a cause larger than himself.

For William, the cause would be to forever remove the blight of slavery from the face of British history. The fight would be long and arduous, demanding every ounce of energy his soul possessed. There would be times of failure and deep depression when it seemed that he would never win this war. John Newton, the redeemed ex-slave trader, would be a source of tremendous encouragement for Wilberforce in those times of discouragement. On the fateful day of February 23, 1807, Wilberforce stepped into the Parliamentary House knowing that this was the day. For more than 40 years, William had led the charge against the slave trade. This day would be the climax of his life's work. At the end of the day, the House passed, by a vote of 283 to 6, to abolish the slave trade. From his deathbed, John Wesley wrote concerning Wilberforce,

> I see not how you can go through your glorious enterprise in opposing that execrable villainy, which is the scandal of religion, of England, and of human nature. Unless God has raised you up for this very thing, you will be worn out by the opposition of men and devils. But if God be for you, who can be against you?[3]

D.L. Moody used to pick up kids in Chicago and give them a penny if they would ride in his horse-drawn wagons to Sunday school. Today, we look up to D.L. Moody. However, if we give a kid a hotdog in our society, people accuse us of bribing them! What's more important? A lousy hotdog that's in your stomach today and in the sewer tomorrow, or a soul that'll be in hell for eternity because it isn't proper to give them a hotdog? If I have to give a kid a hotdog to get him into Sunday school, I'll give him a stinking hotdog. I'm going to do anything that's morally and ethically correct to get kids under the sound of the gospel. Their souls are worth it. You must decide today to commit yourself to the possibilities that are all around you. Give yourself in such a way that will make a difference.

When my mother didn't want me, I felt abandoned and was sure that nobody wanted me. One man just saw a kid sitting on a corner and wanted to help. He didn't have a great love for me because he didn't even know me, but he decided to feed a poor little sheep that day. Because he loved God, he loved a little boy that he really didn't know. So now, when I drive my bus in New York City, you know who I'm picking up—me. I see myself everywhere in this city.

The critics will always be there—they'll always be around. Rather than letting their words drown you in despair, let them fuel you with energy to complete the task. Never forget Nehemiah's words: "No, not today. I'm not coming down. I'm going to finish the job."

Life Principles in the Crosshairs:

- **Dare to make a difference.**
  Can something actually be brought back after being devastated? That is a very relevant question. These self-righteous critics were quick to cast their stones of verbal abuse. It was easy for them to stand on the sidelines, making their snide remarks. It doesn't cost a thing to sit and criticize. Their doubt would be their doom because God can bring back those who have been destroyed. Some of the lives we have touched were on the brink of destruction. Many of these young lives have seen everything by the time they are 11 years old. They've seen it all, and they've been through it all. They have lived in a world of rejection, drugs, violence, abuse, and great pain.

- **Can these stones come to life?**
  When Nehemiah was faced with the pessimistic pounding of these cynical couch potatoes, he had to decide what to do. He knew that once he came off the wall, even

if it was only once, the race would be over. He also knew that he couldn't get involved in a defensive dialogue with the crowd that was trying to divert his attention. Therefore, he decided to ignore them. Just don't talk with the crowd of critics! Let them drown in their sea of skepticism. I have work to do.

- **Attempt great things, accomplish great things.**
  I've survived in New York City because I've learned to ignore people's "advice." When someone tells me to step down and take a rest, I don't do it. Several have taken me to task on this, but I know that if I will just continue to stay on the wall, God somehow will fight the battle for me. Quitting is not an option. Even the most ordinary person can accomplish great things if they refuse give up.

- **Don't quit.**
  The temptation to quit is always strongest when the battle is raging hot and heavy, but what usually marks a winner is his determination to not quit. I've never quit and I'm not going to. I say that publicly to keep myself accountable. So, now I'm stuck. I've had people say, "*If Bill Wilson can keep on going with as much as he's gone through, then so can I.*" They're right! If I can do it, so can you!

- **One can make a difference.**
  The tourist went up to the youth and said, "I know what you're doing and why you're doing it, but there are a couple of miles of beach and thousands of starfish. Do you really think this will make a difference?" The young man looked at him, picked up another starfish and threw it into the surf. "I don't know," he said. "But, it's going to make a difference to this one."

- **You can make a difference.**
  Don't let people discourage you and don't let them question your call, because they will. When you step out of the box and choose to be different, you'll see that "different" doesn't fly in "polite" society. Down through the ages, there have been men and women who defied the odds and went against the stream to accomplish great things.

PART 2

PRINCIPLES FOR CREATING CONSISTENCY

Consistency is an important quality for those who would serve the purposes of God. Samuel Johnson once said that those who attain any excellence commonly spend their lives in one pursuit. Maintaining consistency in your pursuit of your goals is a character trait found in all of those who have succeeded in life.

In this section, I will introduce you to several biblical characters that were forced to face the issue of consistency. As we look at a snippet from the life of Paul, you will learn the value of walking through doors of opportunity. From the life of Moses, you will learn how to avoid the prison of bitterness. Josiah will teach you that you had better not fight the wrong battle. Elimilech will instruct you on a powerful principle of decision-making—never make a decision with one who breaks decisions. Lastly, three tribes of the Jewish nation will teach you the significance of building your own altars in life.

The doors that God opens for you will bring a change in your life and to those you minister to wherever you may go. You will not be able to survive on old manna; you will need fresh manna from God to go through the door. You will need fresh water to minister to new people. You will need to grow and change in order to walk through God's new door in your life.

—Bill Wilson

Opportunity is missed by most people because it is dressed in overalls and looks like work.

—Thomas A. Edison

Small opportunities are often the beginning of great enterprises.

—Demosthenes

CHAPTER 6

WALKING THROUGH DOORS OF OPPORTUNITY

But I will stay on at Ephesus until Pentecost, because a great door for effective work has opened to me, and there are many who oppose me (1 Cor. 16:8-9, NIV).

Paul was willing to wait in the city of Ephesus because a great door of opportunity had opened up for him. Note the sense of urgency in his letter. One can sense how overwhelmed he is as he ponders the possibilities that are before him in this great city. Paul had been in Ephesus for three years and had made plans to go to Macedonia. However, he couldn't shake his sense of responsibility in this city. This critical moment in time required that he seize the opportunity and go through the door. One thing about doors is that they don't always stay open. So, when it is open, you had better go through it.

Paul's urgency was tempered by his obedience. Obedience to God is always more important than our perception of urgency. Remember King Saul? He felt it was more urgent to fight the Philistines than to obey God in waiting for Samuel to come and make the right sacrifice. As such, King Saul missed God's plan for his life. His urgency undermined and shattered his relationship with God. Paul didn't make the same mistake!

Paul could have gone on to Macedonia, and God may have blessed what he did. However, he might have missed a greater opportunity in the city of Ephesus. The door was open and Paul decided to step through. Great men know how to take advantage of open doors.

RECOGNIZING AN OPEN DOOR

When Russia first opened up to the gospel, people began sending Bibles there, and they believed the door would be open forever. Now, the situation has changed. Russia isn't as open now as in the past. Some leaders in the Russian Orthodox Church believe the door is closing. Sometimes, when the door opens, it doesn't mean it will be open forever.

Hong Kong has now become a part of mainland China. The church thought that Hong Kong would always be open, but now, no one knows for sure how long that door will remain open. I believe that the door to Cuba will open soon. When it does, we need to be obedient and go through the door.

I hope that we are all smart enough to know that we must never force a door open and try to go through it in our own strength. God says that it's not by might nor by my power, but "by My Spirit" (Zech. 4:6) that we accomplish His will. Open doors are not made by us or forced open by our own plans and creativity. Rather, they are doors of opportunity opened up by the Spirit of God. A wise man knows how to recognize an open door and has the wisdom to know how to walk through that door.

WHAT WAS THE OPEN DOOR?

The door that opened to Paul in Ephesus was a door of opportunity. Ephesus was a large city, and was at that time the commercial, governmental, and religious capitol of the world. The Temple of Diana, one of the Seven Wonders of the World, was located in Ephesus, and drew thousands of worshipers. Because of the great commerce in this city, it was very wealthy and influential.

The Greek word translated "effective" in 1 Corinthians 16:9 means *active*. Something was happening in Ephesus. In that wide, huge, open door there was great activity going on. Paul had lived in the city for three years and observed the activity and dynamics of the city. He evidently saw a paradigm shift happening that would make the city open for his divine mission. An opportunity was presenting itself to him and Paul would not miss this strategic moment in time.

You have an opportunity right where you are. While you are reading this book, there are opportunities all around you. The key is to be able to see those doors. Often our eyes are blinded to the possibilities that are right before us. Ask God to give you the eyes to be able to see all of the natural opportunities that exist all around you.

I see in my travels all over the world that God is raising up a church in every city, town, community, and village. He is raising up a people who will take His message to the streets and share it with people who aren't like they are—ethnically, economically, culturally, or spiritually. God does build some very interesting and intriguing doors. No door is exactly the same but all have the same purpose—so that we might go through those doors with the message of God's radical love for all people.

What about your door of opportunity?

- What is God calling you to do in your city?

- Do you see hungry people that need to be fed either physically or spiritually?

- Do you see lonesome kids with nowhere to go and nobody to care for them?

- Do you see elderly people that could use a hand getting their groceries home?

Doors of opportunity open right under our noses, but because we are blind to the mundane, ordinary things of life, we often miss them.

I was in Scotland, attending a conference, when a woman came up to me from the Shetland Islands. One hundred ten kids live in the village where she lives, so they bought the Sunday school curriculum, took the principles, listened to a tape, and got started. Of the 110 kids in the whole village, 65 of them are in the Sunday school every week—over 50 percent! It doesn't sound like much if you're only talking about numbers, but in every city, town, community, and village all over this world, God is raising up His Church!

God is raising up a people that will step up to the plate and see the opportunity that's open in their area, and who are determined not to miss it!

THE DOOR OF OBLIGATION

Ephesus was not only a door of opportunity, but it was also a door of obligation. The Greek verb translated "open" in 1 Corinthians 9:16, is in the perfect tense, which indicates that somebody had opened the door for him. Guess what? That somebody was God! God opened it, and when God opens a door, you must move through it because that door will not always stay open. Don't miss it the first time because there may not be a second shot at it.

I'm learning this principle better with each trip I take to Europe. The Europeans have a tremendous heritage in the faith, especially in Scotland and the United Kingdom. You recognize the names: John Knox, John Wesley, and John Whitefield. The problem is that so many European Christians are living on the past and living through their heritage. You can't live in the past. God says in Isaiah,

> "Do not remember the former things, nor consider the things of old. Behold, I will do a new thing, now it shall spring forth; shall you not know it?" (Isa. 43:18-19a, NKJV)

New means "change." *New* means "fresh." The doors that God opens for you will bring a change in your life and those you minister to wherever you may go. You will not be able to survive on old manna; you will need fresh manna from God to go through the door. You will need fresh water to minister to new people. You will need to grow and change in order to walk through God's new door in your life.

It's a new day. Certainly accept your heritage, use it, learn from it, and then move on for the glory of God. It's easy to live on your religious or denominational heritage. It will not help you, and it will not win your community to Jesus Christ. We have an obligation to find creative ways to take advantage of every open door that is around us.

Paul was willing to pay the price because he understood the goal. He was so deeply in love with Christ that there was no sacrifice too great to make on behalf of Him. Paul was willing to do whatever it took because he knew that God had opened the door for him.

Years ago, TV had a game show in which the contestants tried to pick the best prize hidden behind door one, two, or three. God's doors do not exist for your pleasure or choosing. Living in obedience to Him is not a game for you or me. These open doors are not to bring you "fame and glory," and they will come with a price.

Paul told the Romans that he was "…under obligation both to Greeks and to barbarians, both to the wise and to the foolish."[1] He was in debt to God and committed to the preaching of the gospel by all means and in all places.

I'll die being obedient to go through the doors God sets before me. Are you will to sacrifice everything to obey? The obligation set

before you by God's open doors demand your ultimate commitment and sacrifice.

THE DOOR OF OPPOSITION

With the open door came many adversaries. As Paul says,
"and there are many who oppose me." The minute there is an opportunity for God, the devil will be right there knocking at that
same door. In every open door, you will find someone trying to
block your entrance into that door.

Booker T. Washington faced more opposition in his life than
most will ever know, but he learned the secret of dealing with opposition as exemplified in these words: "I have learned that success is to be measured not so much by the position that one has
reached in life as by the obstacles which he has overcome while
trying to succeed."[2]

Why does it seem to bother people so much when things get
rough? People say:

- "Oh, you just don't understand. Things are so hard.
  I have no one to encourage me."

- "The leadership has to approve this and they are
  against me. I can't disobey them."

- "I'm going home excited, but nobody cares. I am
  just one person. What can I do?"

Why does that surprise you? Why does it bother you so much?
Didn't you know that every great feat that has been accomplished
has overcome great odds and opposition? Had I quit at the first
hint of opposition, I never would have gone to New York in the
first place. Everybody said I was foolish going through that door.
I had no denominational support, no financial support, no staff,
and even less sense. I had nothing. Come to think of it, I still have
nothing today. However, I saw a bunch of little kids that were just
like me when I was little. Nobody wanted me either. When my
mother left me on the street corner, she didn't want me. She abandoned me. Because one man stopped—one man cared—I am here
today. His response has inspired me to duplicate his actions many
times over. Don't ever underestimate the power of one simple act
of love.

The doors that are right before you are doors of opportunity and doors of obligation, but I can look straight in your eye and tell you it's also a door of opposition. I've fought every demon imaginable, and they don't always look like drug dealers. They may look like Christians. I have been physically and emotionally beat to a pulp. I have faced financial challenges over and over again. With the open door has come much opposition, but I have also discovered that when there is opposition, it forces me to reevaluate my faith and in turn, I find great grace that will more than match any opposing force.

Just do something a little different and you'll discover how many real friends you've got. When you step out, every devil in hell will come at you. Devils come in all shapes and sizes, including religious ones (see Acts 19).

I really enjoy hanging out with homeless people because if they don't like you they just tell you to go to hell. Because they are so forthright, you know immediately where you stand with them. However, in the church it can be hard to know where you stand. Somebody may want to tell you to go to hell, but they can't because it's against the rules, and you may want to tell them the same thing, but you know you can't. So, instead, you just say, "God bless you," because that's all you can say. We cover up all our feelings with such religious piety that it will almost be impossible to get the job done. Our religiosity creates great barriers in the doors of opportunity that God has opened up for us.

C.S. Lewis said the only problem he had with Christianity was Christians. Gandhi said, I like your Christ, I do not like your Christians. Your Christians are so unlike your Christ. There is something very sad in those words.

Paul said there are many adversaries. He fought the Sanhedrin, the religious elite, more than he fought anybody else. In every city, they were there to oppose him. You too will probably meet adversaries as soon as you begin to implement these principles. When you do, don't give up. Instead, pray, be persistent, and lean into God's grace. The only way you will miss out on the opportunity God sets before you is if you quit.

LIFE PRINCIPLES IN THE CROSSHAIRS:

- **God opens doors of opportunity.**
  Don't push the doors open in your own strength. Follow God's lead. Remember that obedience to God's way and

timing is more important than your personal sense of urgency.

- **Doors of opportunity are also doors of obligation.**
  The obligation moves you beyond what's comfortable, traditional, or familiar. God is doing a new thing. Are you ready for it?

- **Doors of opposition are part of the package.**
  Don't be surprised if your greatest opposition comes from the church instead of the world. Don't let opposition discourage or deter you. When you patiently move forward, pray, be persistent, and lean into the grace of God. So, don't quit! Go through that open door.

Do you know how not to get disillusioned? Don't get "illusioned" or idealistic. Being illusioned means that we have unrealistic expectations of ourselves and others. I recognize that people will be people with the good, the bad, and the ugly all mixed in together. People can be unthinking and say hurtful and cruel things. We must move beyond these petty things and keep on with the vision. Bitterness will only imprison you and keep you from the vision.

—Bill Wilson

Hanging onto resentment is letting someone you despise live rent-free in your head.

—Ann Landers

Bitterness imprisons life; love releases it. Bitterness paralyzes life; love empowers it. Bitterness sours life; love heals it. Bitterness blinds life; love anoints its eye.

—Harry Fosdick

CHAPTER 7

AVOID THE PRISON OF BITTERNESS

Then Moses led Israel from the Red Sea and they went into the Desert of Shur. For three days they traveled in the desert without finding water. When they came to Marah, they could not drink its water because it was bitter. (That is why the place is called Marah.) So the people grumbled against Moses, saying, "What are we to drink?" Then Moses cried out to the Lord, and the Lord showed him a piece of wood. He threw it into the water, and the water became sweet. There the Lord made a decree and a law for them, and there He tested them. He said, "If you listen carefully to the voice of the Lord your God and do what is right in His eyes, if you pay attention to His commands and keep all His decrees, I will not bring on you any of the diseases I brought on the Egyptians, for I am the Lord, who heals you." Then they came to Elim, where there were twelve springs and seventy palm trees, and they camped there near the water (Exod. 15:22-27, NIV).

After the triumph over Egypt at the Red Sea, Israel went immediately into the desert. I have noticed that, often in life, right after our greatest successes we are often faced with our greatest trial. No victory will ever secure us forever against trials and testing. The rhythm of triumph and testing create the cadence, orchestrating our journey though life.

FROM BLESSING TO BITTERNESS

In a state of ecstasy they joyously continued the journey away from the place of victory. With the Red Sea in their rear view mirror, they arrived at the hot sands of the Arabian Desert. For three days now they have been traveling with the sun mercilessly beating down on their backs and the hot sand scorching their feet. The stinging sand created by the hot, arid winds flogs their faces. Their water has run out and their mouths are parched as dehydration sets in. Blisters are forming on their lips. You know the story.

Finally, they reach a place called Marah. As they crest the hill and see the waters of Marah, their despair turns to great delight. Their rejoicing is a bit too soon. As the first Israelis scoop up the water into their mouths, they violently cough and spew the water out, because it is dreadfully bitter. The Hebrew word Marah means "bitter," so the place was called *Marah* because the water was bitter.

The children of Israel allowed the bitterness of the water to create a bitterness in their souls. They became disheartened and angry with Moses. They had already forgotten how God had delivered them in the waters of the Red Sea. Some of them were ready to quit and go back to Egypt. Others just said, "Forget it. If this is what God has planned for me, I don't want it." In spite of their gross lack of faith, God performed a miracle there on the desert sands, turning bitter waters into sweet waters.

Don't miss this principle! Often, when our lives plummet into distress, fashioned by the entrance of baffling predicaments, we are tempted to crumble into despair and bitterness. We lash out at the perceived source of our struggles, whether it is God or those around us. We say, "If this is what God has for me, I don't want it. If this is what God has brought me to, I don't want it."

There is a powerful secret that I have learned that may help at this point of the journey. *If God brings you out of something, He will bring you into something better. He will bring you from the bitter place to a better place.* Sometimes, to get to the place where God wants to bless us, we have to pass through situations that can produce bitterness in our soul. The key is to overcome the bitterness—created by the prevailing winds of opposition—by focusing on the promises of blessing and support that will come to us.

MOVING FROM THE PLACE OF BITTERNESS TO THE PLACE OF BLESSING

The second place they stopped was a place called Elim. Elim was a *better* place. Elim was the total opposite from Marah. The Bible says it was very green because there were 12 fresh water springs and 70 palm trees. It was an oasis and a place of refreshing. God always has a secret place of refreshing that will help you survive the bitter places in your life.

Many of the Israelites got discouraged at Marah. Some of them wanted to quit and turn back. However, what most people don't know is that *Elim was only seven miles from Marah!* Seven miles! Your greatest opportunity for deliverance might just be a small distance from your greatest time of distress.

If you're going to go to the next level, if you're going to accomplish something for God, never forget this principle. The attitude that you need to complete the journey from bitterness to blessing is perseverance. Failure is often the early morning dawn after darkness, right before the rising sun of success. It is perseverance that enables us to meet the rising sun.

This perseverance must be a determination that is founded in God's grace and not our own human strength. If not, that resolve will burn up into "burnout" as we deplete our own human resources.

BURNING YOUR BOATS BEHIND YOU

When the ancient Romans landed in a new country for the purpose of conquering it, they unloaded the boats and burned them. The Romans burned the boats. If the soldiers became discouraged, too bad! They had no choice now but to advance and win the battles because there was no way of escape. They couldn't run away when the battle grew intense all around them. They had to stay and fight. They had no choice; their boats were burned.

What do you need to burn so that you will not look back? What way of escape have you left open? When the going gets tough, have you left yourself an exit strategy? If so, then you need to burn your boats and retreat plans. When the battle rages around you and you are in the midst of great conflict, you can survive if you have determination in your soul, passion in your heart, and are committed to your God-given destiny.

I don't have a retreat plan because I've never left one for myself. I have done this on purpose. I have said to others in the past, "I'm not leaving New York." Why have I said this? I'm painting myself into a corner. I'm not trying to be brash, nor am I trying to impress others. But when I say I'm doing this for the rest of my life, it doesn't leave me any out. I have burned my boats. I refuse to turn back. I'm not going away. I am here to stay. Retreat is not an option.

ONLY SEVEN MILES TO YOUR NEXT SUCCESS

Elim was only seven miles farther. You may ask, "But how did they know?" That's the whole point! You're not going to know unless you just keep moving forward. You've got to keep going. You can stop at any point along this road if you want. You can roll your eyes and get angry with your enemies, bitter about your circumstances, and frustrated because you see no solution in sight. Or, you can set your face towards the rising sun and keep moving forward. The principle of success is built on the foundation of determination. Alexander Graham Bell wrote about this unusual power of determination with these words: "What this power is I cannot say; all I know is that it exists and it becomes available only when a man is in that state of mind in which he knows exactly what he wants and is fully determined not to quit until he finds it."[1]

You can allow your present challenging circumstances to be a roadblock, or you can decide to remove that roadblock and keep moving. You can choose to move on from the place of bitterness knowing that your place of blessing is only seven miles away.

THREE KEYS TO UNDERSTANDING BITTERNESS AND BLESSING

These are three extremely critical observations that will help you understand the curse of bitterness and the corridor that leads to blessing.

Observation #1: When you get to the place of bitterness, keep on going.

Don't unpack your bags! Yes, you're tired; I am too. Yes, you're discouraged; so am I. Are you surprised that I get discouraged? People think I like to fight but I just look like a fighter. I come across like that; it fits with the New York mind-set. But, I don't like to fight. I get tired just like everybody else. I have had my times of discouragement and bitterness. I don't go looking for a fight, but neither would I run away from a fight. I learned a long time ago that if this were easy, everybody would be doing what I do. I just keep moving forward, knowing that the scenery will change.

Nobody in the history of the United States has ever done what we've done in ministering to kids. The concepts we have developed are being duplicated all over the world because they are based upon sound biblical principles that can be transferred into any place. You can't duplicate a personality like Robert Schuller or

Billy Graham, but you can duplicate principles. Metro Ministries is not built on personality; it's built on transferable principles.

They are biblical principles that transcend cultures, denominations, race, and generations. People of all denominations, in all countries, and in all facets of life, are applying these principles all over the world. These principles have been built upon the principle of dogged determination.

There is always a tomorrow, so keep on going. Yes, you'll get discouraged because it's hard and it can be frustrating. With the victories will always come greater challenges that will lead you to the next level. But the principle remains the same. Keep going on. In our ministry, we constantly look at how many kids we want to reach. Every one of our sidewalk Sunday school trucks works with 1,000 kids. With three full-time people assigned to Sunday school trucks who are ministering seven days a week, we know that we can bring in 2,000 more kids. We envision the possibilities and then work to make them come true.

I wonder what would happen if you had a vision of the possibilities for ministry that exist all around you. I wonder what would happen if you started reaching out to the children and teenagers in your own neighborhood. I wonder what would happen if you reached out to those on your streets in the form of basic, godly compassion. I wonder what would happen if someone really cared!

People come to New York and see how things can be and the Spirit of God empowers them with their own vision. However, it's not just a New York thing, nor is it just a Metro thing. It's certainly not a Bill Wilson thing; it's a Jesus thing. That's why the principles of this ministry are going all over the world. Normal, everyday people see the possibilities for their own city and are willing to cross the line and get out of the box.

If you want something you've never had before, you're going to have to do something you've never done. If you want something different, quit doing the same stuff. Get out of the box—cross the line! Do something different.

Observation #2: You can go from trials to triumph at any time. It's your choice.

How do you get from Marah to Elim? When you get angry, frustrated, and tired of fighting, you just determine that you must get back on the road to Elim. There are many things you can do to get your mind off the mess and back into the fight, including:

- Go visit the little ones in the AIDS baby ward. Just sit there with a bunch of little babies that will die unless God performs a miracle.

- Walk around the streets of your city and see if God just might speak to you.

- Visit someone in prison, a nursing home, or the hospital.

Once you get your eyes off of your "Marah," place of bitterness, you just might be on the road to "Elim," your place of blessing. It isn't that far, you know!

Observation #3: It is only Seven miles back to the place of bitterness.

Marah is as close to Elim as Elim is to Marah. It was only seven miles from Marah to Elim, so guess what? It's only seven miles back. Many times, I've seen youth workers doing a great work, but all of a sudden, they get their feelings hurt. They get disillusioned with church or with their situation and just want to give up. So what! Anytime we work with people, we will become disappointed. People often don't think, and end up saying hurtful and cruel things. The key is not to allow the words of criticism to sink into your heart and damper the fires of passion in your soul. We must move beyond petty things in ministry and keep on with the vision.

Do you know how to avoid disillusionment? Don't get "illusioned" in the first place. Being "illusioned" means that we have unrealistic expectations of ourselves and others. I must recognize that people will be people—with the good, the bad, and the ugly all mixed in together. The rash and reckless people in church are like the poor—they'll be with us always. Therefore, don't get rattled and don't get offended when their words or actions hurt you. Successful people have learned to rise above the debris that exists in the backwash of jealousy, criticism, and anger that often will oppose us in our journey to fulfill our destinies.

I once had an evangelist that put me on his TV show to help me raise money for the ministry. He put me on his telethon for one week, and we raised over twelve million dollars. Do you know how much came to me for the ministry? Zero! Zero! Was I bitter? You bet, I was real bitter. The FCC called me twice from Washington to come testify against him but I wouldn't do it. I don't play that game because nobody wins. The only person that a bitter spirit hurts is the person harboring that spirit.

I learned a long time ago, what goes around comes around. If you sit by the river long enough, you'll get a chance to see your enemies float by. You just have to sit there long enough. I saw that old boy going by not too long ago. The best way to handle disappointment is perseverance. You just hang in there; you do right; you slug it out; you keep a sweet spirit.

I refuse to live in bitterness. I've visited it a few times. I've even stayed in the Marah Hilton a few times, a little angry and bitter. But, you know what? I'm not going to live there. I know that I must pack my bags, check out of that place, and get on down the road where a better place is waiting for me.

LIFE PRINCIPLES IN THE CROSSHAIRS:

- **Move from the place of bitterness to the place of blessing.**
  Your greatest opportunity for deliverance might just be a small distance from your greatest time of distress. If you're going to go to the next level, if you're going to accomplish something for God, never forget this principle. The attitude that you need to complete the journey from bitterness to blessing is perseverance. Failure is often that early morning dawn after darkness, right before the rising sun of success. It is perseverance that enables us to meet the rising sun.

- **Burn your boats behind you.**
  I don't have a retreat plan because I've never left one for myself. I have said to others in the past, "I'll die doing this ministry." Why have I said this? I'm painting myself into a corner. I'm not trying to be cool, nor am I trying to impress others. But when I say I'm doing this for the rest of my life, it doesn't leave me any way out. I have burned my boats.

- **It is only seven miles back to the place of bitterness.**
  The rash and reckless people in church are like the poor—they'll be with us always. Therefore, don't get

rattled and don't get offended when their words or actions hurt you. Successful people have learned to rise above the debris that exists in the backwash of jealousy, criticism, and anger that often will oppose us in our journey to fulfill our destinies.

Being a victim is a sickness—it makes everyone around you sick but at some point in your life, you've got to grow up and be responsible for yourself. It's time to be responsible for your decisions, your actions, and your life and how you choose to live it.

—Bill Wilson

Every great mistake has a halfway moment, a split second when it can be recalled and perhaps remedied.

—Pearl Buck

Since the social victim has been oppressed by society, he comes to feel that his individual life will be improved more by changes in society than by his own initiative. Without realizing it, he makes society rather than himself the agent of change. The power he finds in his victimization may lead him to collective action against society, but it also encourages passivity within the sphere of his personal life.

—Shelby Steele

CHAPTER **8**

DON'T FIGHT THE WRONG BATTLES

How old do you have to get before you stop making stupid mistakes? Evidently, pretty old for a lot of people. I have seen a lot of people old enough to know better still run off, half-baked, and wind up shooting themselves in the foot. It seems like the only decision they know how to make is a foolish one. In order to make smart decisions, you are required to:

- Stop and carefully consider the options that are available to you.

- Look around and consider what others have done in similar circumstances.

- Listen to the advice of wise counselors with proven success.

You need to understand that every decision you make in life will not only affect your life, but also, it will affect the lives that are closest to you. The larger the organization, the more lives that will be affected by your decisions.

IT'S NOT ME—IT'S THEE

You know the story. When Josiah was eight, he became the king of Israel, and ruled for thirty-one years. Though Josiah was young, he sought the counsel of older priests and became a very wise young man. He knew the principle of "stop, look, and listen." Josiah's father, Amon, was a wicked king. He hadn't followed the precepts of God and he led the people of God into the wicked practice of worshiping idols. Josiah's grandfather, Manasseh, was even worse. Not only had he turned the hearts of the people toward idol worship, but he also put an idol of Asherah in the Temple. The Bible says that he led the people to do even worse things than the heathen Amorites had done. What an ancestry for young Josiah: a wicked father and super-wicked grandfather. In spite of some really bad genes, Josiah did pretty well and ruled Israel as a gracious king. He could have made a lot of excuses for his past, blaming his family for a poor example. He did not blame anyone, but simply followed the ways of the Lord.

Our culture is full of blame-shifting and excuse-making. How often do you turn on your TV set and see some daytime TV program with people acting like fools, airing their dirty laundry in front of the nation and the world? These people say outrageous things like: "When I was three my mother dropped me on my head, that's why I'm an idiot."

No, you're an idiot because you're an idiot! It has nothing to do with your mother dropping you on your head. You make your own choices in life and then gripe about the consequences. You decide to act stupid and then wonder why stupid things happen to you!

The company of psychologists in this country has only fed into the problem. For fifty years, people have been perfecting the craft of being a victim. Blame-shifting has been perfected into a fine art. All of this self-justification has weakened our character and prevented us from maturing into adults who are able to take responsibility for the decisions that we make.

Being a victim is a sickness—it makes everyone around you sick. At some point in your life, you've got to grow up and be responsible for yourself. It's time to be responsible for your decisions, your actions, and overall, for how you choose to live your life.

As you begin to mature, you will no longer hesitate in making decisions, but you will need to learn a very important lesson as you shift your focus from excuse-making to decision-making. If you are preparing to cross this line, get out of the box and do something different, then you must learn this principle well: Don't fight in the wrong battles!

FIGHTING THE WRONG BATTLES

Though Josiah came from a heritage of wickedness, he had fulfilled his kingly responsibilities with honor and dignity. During his time as king, he was committed to destroying the idol worship amongst his people and tearing down the high places where they had worshiped them. He rid the nation of false prophets, repaired the temple, and cleaned out the house of God. He successfully reinstated the worship of Jehovah in Judah.

Not all mistakes are the same. Some are more costly than others. For many people, their last mistake is the most costly.

- The skydiver who didn't check his 'chute—it didn't open as he plummeted to the ground.

- The truck driver who didn't check his tires—one blew out and he was in a tragic accident.

- The carpenter who didn't check his ladder—it broke at a rotten part as he was climbing up to the rooftop.

For Josiah, his last mistake was very costly. It was costly not only for him, but for his entire army and the nation as well. Let's see what happened:

> *After all this, when Josiah had prepared the temple, Necho king of Egypt came up to fight against Carchemish by the Euphrates; and Josiah went out against him. But he sent messengers to him, saying, "What have I to do with you, king of Judah? I have not come against you this day, but against the house with which I have war; for God commanded me to make haste. Refrain from meddling with God, who is with me, lest He destroy you." Nevertheless Josiah would not turn his face from him, but disguised himself so that he might fight with him, and did not heed the words of Necho from the mouth of God. So he came to fight in the Valley of Megiddo. And the archers shot King Josiah; and the king said to his servants, "Take me away, for I am severely wounded." His servants therefore took him out of that chariot and put him in the second chariot that he had, and they brought him to Jerusalem. So he died, and was buried in one of the tombs of his fathers. And all Judah and Jerusalem mourned for Josiah* (2 Chron. 35:20-24, NKJV).

Josiah did something that he never should have done. Necho, the king of Egypt, went to war against Carchemish, over by the Euphrates River. The problem was that Josiah thought Necho was coming against him in the battle, as well. So, Josiah prepared himself to go to war against Necho. Upon seeing Josiah's advance into battle, Necho told Josiah that he was going to fight Carchemish, not Judah. We have no clue about why Josiah did not believe him, but he didn't. Josiah persisted in going against Necho. As Necho was passing through, Josiah met him in battle in the Valley of Megiddo. It was there, during the battle, that Josiah was mortally wounded and died a tragic death. A life that had been so promising was lost in a senseless battle.

AVOID UNNECESSARY CASUALTIES

Josiah died in a war that he never should have fought in the first place. There was absolutely no reason for him to be on that battlefield. It was a bad decision. He did not stop, look, and listen. I wonder how many churches, how many Christians, how many folks have died in battles in which they never should have fought. Many leaders haven't been taught the most basic rule of engagement: Choose your battles wisely. Often we create problems and situations that never should have been created. Normally, this is because of pride, impatience, foolishness, and because we wrongly evaluated the situation.

The next time you're faced with a battle decision, ask yourself these questions:

- Is it worth the fight?
- Is it worth what can be lost?
- Is it worth what can be gained?

RULES OF ENGAGEMENT

Every war zone has its clear rules of engagement. If you violate those rules, it can be costly. Failure to heed these rules will lead to battlefields being littered with the dead and dying casualties of unnecessary wars.

Observation #1: Sometimes what you think is your friend is actually your enemy.

Don't get so caught up in the battle that you lose sight of the war. Good ideas may not be God ideas. If they aren't from God, they'll deplete you energies and cause unnecessary casualties. Let me give you some examples.

I know of churches that wanted a Christian school. Is a Christian school a good battle? Absolutely. Is it the main battle? No, it's not. Furthermore, I know churches that have gone bankrupt trying to have a Christian school. A good idea is not necessarily a God idea.

I know of churches that started a television ministry. Is Christian TV good? Yes. Is it a good battle? Yes. Is it the war? No. I know churches that have gone bankrupt because they were so committed to getting on TV that they destroyed their ministry in the effort.

I know of a pastor who thought abortion was wrong. Is abortion wrong? Of course it is. Is it a battle to fight? Sure. Is it the entire war? No.

It's much easier to go handcuff yourself to the doors of an abortion clinic so you can get on CNN, than to get acquainted with those young girls, walk them through the nine months of pregnancy, help them out, counsel them, and try to get the baby adopted. That's a long-term commitment. Some would rather aim at being on CNN than make a long-term commitment. Sometimes the battles we engage ourselves in are a diversion to avoid the real commitments we should be making.

Is fighting against abortion a good battle? Yes, it's a good battle. Is it the war? No, it's not the war. The real war is reaching these young girls and helping them begin to make wise decisions rather than foolish ones.

Sometimes what you think is your friend can be your enemy. You need to be careful how you engage every issue of life. Learn to make wise decisions that are based upon prayer and the wise counsel of others.

Observation # 2: Sometimes what you think is your enemy can be your friend.

I'll use my traveling as an example. I hate traveling. I've traveled every week for 21 years because I have to raise money to keep the ministry going, but I hate it. I'm tired of traveling, I'm tired of airports, and I'm really tired of peanuts and pretzels. I've eaten more peanuts and pretzels than any man should ever eat in three lifetimes.

For a long time, I thought traveling was my enemy. But, now that I'm older, I've learned that if I had stayed home and did not travel, I would not have trained the leadership that I have surrounding me today. Why? If I were there all the time, I would run it. However, because I'm forced to leave every week to raise the money for the huge expenses of the ministry, they are forced to handle the work while I am gone. Therefore, because I've had to travel, it has forced me to train leadership. What I thought was my enemy turned out to be my friend.

THANK GOD FOR UNANSWERED PRAYER

I used to hate country music when I was young, but now that I'm older, I'm starting to like it. That's a scary thing in itself. Garth Brooks has a song, "Thank God for Unanswered Prayer." There is such a powerful truth in the lyrics of that song. Sometimes we pray for things that we really don't need. Our prayers are often motivated by fear, emotions, selfish desires, or anger. We are very blessed that God does not answer every prayer that we pray. Some of us have prayed some really bad prayers that were not worthy to be answered. "And when His disciples James and John saw this, they said, 'Lord, do You want us to command fire to come down from heaven and consume them...?'" (Luke 9:54, NKJV) Now there is a prayer that should not be answered.

Have you ever been in a situation that looked like it would never end? I can tell you that over the twenty-five years I've been in New York City, many times I've prayed for things that, later, I was glad God didn't do.

When I was twenty-five, I almost got married. I thought I was in love. This was serious stuff. I thought this was it. We got the engagement ring; we went apartment hunting, and did the whole routine that engaged couples do.

One night, I went over to her house. When I got there, she told me that she decided she couldn't live this kind of life. I suppose not many women could. She said, "I can't do this!" and threw the ring at me. It took me an hour to find it; I wasn't going to let that go. Recently, I was in Dallas and saw her at a convention, and I thought to myself, "Thank God for unanswered prayer!" It's amazing what 25 years will do.

If God answered every prayer that we utter, what a mess we would have. Only God knows what's best for us. And we think we're so smart. It is best to allow our prayers to flow from a heart that simply wants Father's will to be done and not ours. Remember, this is how our Lord taught us to pray: "Thy kingdom come. Thy will be done on earth as it is in heaven." Hopefully, the older you become, you will be able to discern a good friend from a real enemy.

Life Principles in the crosshairs:

- **Stop—look—listen.**
  In order to make smart decisions you must stop and carefully consider the options that are available to you, look around and consider what others have done in similar circumstances, and listen to the advice of wise counselors with proven success.

- **It's not me—it's thee.**
  Being a victim is a sickness—it makes everyone around you sick. At some point in your life, you've got to grow up and be responsible for yourself. It's time to be responsible for your decisions, your actions, and how you choose to live your life.

- **Fighting the wrong battles.**
  Josiah did something that he shouldn't have done. Necho, the king of Egypt, went to war against Carchemish, over by the Euphrates River. The problem was, Josiah thought Necho was coming to fight him. However, Necho told Josiah that he was going to fight Carchemish, but for some reason, Josiah didn't believe him. As Necho was passing through, Josiah met him in battle in the Valley of Megiddo. It was there, during the battle, that Josiah was mortally wounded, and died.

- **Avoid unnecessary casualties.**
  Don't miss this! Josiah died in a war that he never should have fought in the first place. I wonder how many churches, how many Christians, and how many folks have died in battles they never should have fought. Many leaders haven't been taught the most basic rule of engagement: Choose your battles wisely.

- **Rules of engagement.**
  Every war zone has its clear rules of engagement. If you violate those rules, it can be costly. Failure to follow the rules leads to battlefields being littered with the dead and dying casualties of unnecessary wars.

There are right and wrong times to make important decisions. We think if the sun's not shining where we are, then we need to go where it is shining. We conclude that adversity in the place where we are is wrong and therefore presume that it is time for a change. Your erratic emotions and personal perceptions are not always good guides for making accurate decisions.

—Bill Wilson

Vacillating people seldom succeed. Successful men and women are very careful in reaching their decisions, and very persistent and determined in action thereafter.

—L. G. Elliott

It is the characteristic excellence of the strong man that he can bring momentous issues to the fore and make a decision about them. The weak are always forced to decide between alternatives they have not chosen themselves.

—Dietrich Bonhoeffer

Chapter 9

Don't Make a Decision
With a Broken Decision Maker

Making decisions is a basic part of the process of life. Good decision-making requires a mixture of skills: creative development and identification of options, clarity of judgment, firmness, and effective implementation. Problem-solving often involves decision-making, which is especially important to those who aspire to any form of leadership. It is important to understand the different factors involved in making good and bad decisions. There are right and wrong times to make decisions.

For example, don't ever make decisions when you're not in a position to make spiritual, rational, intelligent decisions. Before making any decision, one must learn to connect with God's Spirit in order to find the wisdom that will guide him in making the right decisions. Making the right decision and implementing it in the right way, for the right reason, and at the right time, determines success. Often, wrong decisions are made when we are in crisis mode just trying to cope with the swirl of negativity all around us.

Making Decisions With a Broken Decision Maker

In the Book of Ruth, we read about a couple that made a decision with a broken decision maker. Because of a great famine, Elimelech and Naomi left Israel and headed to the land of Moab. They evidently felt like they were forced by their circumstances to go to a place where they could find work in order to meet all of their physical needs. They were only going to be there for a little while, but time rolled on and eventually, Elimelech and his sons all died in that strange land far away from the land of promise. Only Naomi and her two daughters-in-law were left. They originally planned on sojourning through there. It never works out that way.

There are times in your life when you're just not equipped or emotionally prepared to make decisions. Often, in the midst of crisis, we are forced to make the wrong decisions, and we end up paying the price. One of the biggest challenges of leadership is determining the right process for making good and lasting decisions.

I remember when a former staff member came up to me after a service and said he was sorry that he had left Metro. The problem was not *that* he had left, but *how* he had left. He had left in a way that he couldn't come back. I can't emphasize this enough: If you have to leave somewhere, leave the right way. Don't burn the bridge you are crossing, because you may have to come back across that bridge some day.

I have had my share of successes and failures when it comes to making decisions. In fact, life involves learning how to make better decisions as a result of your victories and defeats. In the process of making hundreds of decisions over the years, I have learned some very important keys for effective decision-making, usually the hard way.

EIGHT OBSERVATIONS FOR EFFECTIVE DECISION-MAKING

There are right and wrong times to make important decisions. We think, if the sun's not shining where we are, then we need to go where it is shining. We conclude, when adversity hits in the place where we are, that something must be wrong, and therefore, we presume that it is time for a change. Your erratic emotions and personal perceptions are not always good guides for making accurate decisions. However, the biggest mistake I've witnessed is when people try to make important, life-changing decisions when they're in no position to do so. Here are a few tips for when you should not be making a life-changing decision:

Observation # 1: Don't make the decision when you're discouraged.

The day of the week that most preachers choose to resign from ministry is Monday. It's because they're fed up with people problems they have experienced on Sunday. Also, it seems that extreme highs are followed by extreme lows. Sometimes, our greatest successes are followed by times of great discouragement. The great victory that Elijah had at Mt. Carmel was followed by a season of extreme discouragement.

It's hard to be objective when you are on the bottom of a pit. Disappointments followed by despair create a cloud of confusion that makes it difficult to think rationally. Don't make decisions on Monday. Refuse to make a decision when you're discouraged! Be patient and allow the pain created by the crisis to subside. Leave yourself time to bleed. I used to bleed for a week. Now I've got it down to a day, but it's taken years. Allow yourself time to become spiritually refreshed and time for the mist of chaos to lift. Then, you will be able to experience the ability to focus on your situation with greater clarity and conviction.

Observation # 2: Don't make a decision when you're not right with God.

If you're not right with God, do not make a life-changing decision. Have you ever noticed that, when someone's personal life starts getting off track, the first thing they do is quit church? Before being too judgmental, you need to realize that the reason this happens is because they don't want to face the critics. Someone once said that the Church is the only army that kills its wounded. I couldn't agree more.

It's unfortunate, but many Christians don't demonstrate the radical grace of Jesus in such a way that will bring people back into the Kingdom. They find it easier to gossip and criticize, rather than keep their own lives straight. Too often, the very people that can't run their own lives will tell you how to run yours. Their own lives are heading toward disaster. Nonetheless, they try to tell you what to do. The blind cannot lead the blind. Don't listen to the advice of others when their lives are not right with God.

When you're not right with God, it's not the time to make life-changing decisions. When, at some point in your life, you have taken a detour that led you to a dead end, you must be careful. This is not the time to panic and start making all kinds of crazy decisions. When you don't feel connected to God, it is not the right time to initiate decisions that could just lead you further away. So, what do you do? You follow, as they say in the army, the last given command. Trace your steps backward and see if you can locate the place where you deviated and took the path of your own choosing. Also, don't give up just because you failed and now feel abandoned. Just hang in there. When the Bible talks about encountering trials, the advice the author gives is "endure." "No temptation has overtaken you but such as is common to man; and God is faithful, who will not allow you to be tempted beyond what you are able, but with the temptation will provide the way of escape, also, so that you will be able to endure it" (1 Cor. 10:13, NASB).

Stay in the presence of God and keep close to those who love God. You cannot hear God's voice unless you are in His presence and staying close to those who love Him. In that positive environment, you will begin to recover and reconnect with your Father.

Observation # 3: Don't make a decision when you're homesick.

At Metro, we have staff members from all over the world. For about the first month, they're fine, but then they hear the gunshots in the middle of the night, and they begin to realize that they are in a war zone. Then, they find out that the food's not so good. Then, they get a letter from home, "We miss you baby." Pretty soon you see it; they start getting homesick. The tug of a safe and normal environment begins to pull on the strings of their hearts.

God has taken or will take you to a place that is new, different, and difficult. It could be across town or halfway around the world. Just because you don't like your surroundings, you have no reason to make decisions that will remove you from your difficult environment. Your circumstances and environment don't determine where you live—God does. When you're homesick, it is not the time to make a decision. You will often find yourself in situations that are not comfortable. Often, these places can be times of great stretching. The linings of your soul will never be stretched in the soft and secure places of the "known." We get enlarged and strengthened when we get into unfamiliar territory, working with different people. These are not the times to make rash decisions and retreat.

Observation # 4: Don't make a big decision when you're angry.

Barnabas and Paul had made a dynamic duo, and in their travels, they were effectively pushing the Kingdom into virgin territory. Unfortunately, this partnership came to a tragic end. A heated argument had developed between Barnabas and Paul about taking John Mark on the next journey (see Acts 15:36-41). Barnabas declared that if John Mark didn't go, then he wouldn't either. It's interesting that we don't hear from Barnabas again. What did Barnabas do? He made a decision with a broken decision maker.

Anger creates a heavy haze in your spirit that can darken your perspective. Remember, your perception isn't always reality. God's perception is reality, not yours. Give your angry feelings time to ventilate in constructive ways. Anger is a lot like a cloudy windshield in your car. When hot air on the inside has hit the cold glass, it forms a mist on the windshield that keeps you from seeing clearly. But, if you roll down a window or balance the temperature in the car with the outside air, the windshield clears and you can accurately see what's in front of you. This is what you have to do with anger. You need other people to help you balance your perspective and, most of all, you need time in the presence of Father to just chill out and bring your temperature down.

Don't let anger cloud the windshield of your perception. Give yourself some time to let the anger subside. Scripture counsels us not to go to bed with anger, and to be angry, but not to sin (see Eph. 4:26). Let go of your anger constructively before you make a major decision.

One of the awesome things about God is that failure is never final. Even though this dynamic duo of Paul and Barnabas was broken apart by John Mark, later on Paul writes to Timothy: "Only Luke is with me. Pick up Mark and bring him with you, for he is useful to me for service" (2 Tim. 4:11, NASB). This does not invalidate the principle. Anger will lead you to wrong places and is the seedbed for bad decisions. That, in my experience, takes people to a place they cannot come back from.

Observation # 5: Don't make a decision when you're sick.

You're not competent to make good decisions while you're being attacked by illness. When you are sick, your resistance is down. Moreover, you're upset, frustrated, and rattled. Your focus is off, and the pain of your infirmity will prevent you from rational thought. It's not the time. Sickness drains your body and mind of the natural resources needed to make appropriate decisions. You can't think clearly. What you need to do is to recover physically before you try to act mentally. Get well. Take care of your body. Be patient and allow yourself to mend physically before you make those key decisions in your life.

Observation # 6: Don't make a decision when you're enticed with something that you want to do.

It is easy to make the wrong decision when you're enticed with something you want to do. Lust, in any form, can be a serious distraction.

Once I was yelling at the garbage men that the high price of collection was "killing" me. It costs two to three hundred dollars per month for garbage collection, so I was complaining. They asked me if I was having financial difficulties, and I said, "Yes." When they left, they said they would see what they could do about it. Several days later, two men in suits came to my office. They said that they understood I was having financial difficulties and wanted to try and help. I thought, "Ok. What do these guys want?" One of them put a briefcase on my desk and opened it to reveal ten thousand dollars cash! This was turning into a movie. They said one of their "constituents" wanted to offer me this donation. Well I'll tell you, I looked at that ten grand and my mind began to spin. I only could imagine what I could do with that money. There were so many places that it could be used in the ministry. I asked what they wanted in return, and they said that all they wanted was a receipt for twenty thousand dollars. That's all, just a receipt.

I quickly asked God if I could take it and then immediately asked for forgiveness. Right is right and wrong is wrong. I could not violate my conscience, even though I really needed that money. But, to be truthful, when you start dealing with people like that, it never ends. Sure, we could have used the money, but it would have been the wrong thing to do. In the end, I declined the offer and asked the men to leave, and that was the end of it. It could have gone either way.

Never make a decision while you are being enticed with something you want. It will come back to haunt you every time.

Observation # 7: Don't make a decision when you're passionate.

Don't make a decision when you're fired up with passion. When passions are running high, your ability to think is impaired. It's hard to count to ten when passion is high, so what makes you think you can make a big decision? Have you ever tried to walk away in the heat of an argument? It's not easy, is it? It's much easier to walk away before the passion runs high and you haven't been insulted. Just try it sometime, you'll see.

When your passions are high, too many other chemicals are flowing through your blood stream. This fire of passion obscures all that is real around you. You start to see opportunities that are not really there, and you can miss the danger lurking just around the corner. Why do you think so many first or second date marriages fail? These people are good people, but their decision making is impaired. They were in lust, not in love. How can you love someone that you've just met? He or she may be an axe murderer just looking for another victim—and you're it! Passion has a way of making us a little goofy and subject to really bad decisions.

Back off, and let passions cool down. This is where it is really important to have trustworthy friends in your life to help you see accurately when passion has blurred your vision.

Observation # 8: Don't make a decision when you're impatient.

In a moment of great impatience, Abraham and Sarah made a very bad decision (see Gen. 16). Thinking that the promise of God was never going to come to pass, they took matters into their own hands. The result—Ishmael. Good ideas are not necessarily God ideas. Their impatience created a disastrous result that we are still dealing with today. The problems in the Middle East are descended from the bad decisions first made by Abraham and Sarah. Abraham and Sarah made a decision with a broken decision maker. They got impatient and took matters into their own hands and now we are paying the price.

To prevent this, get some godly advice from someone whose decision maker is working. This could be an older, spiritually mature Christian, your pastor, or someone that you trust. Patience in decision making is critical.

LIFE PRINCIPLES IN THE CROSSHAIRS:

- **Take time to consider your choices carefully.**
  Don't rush into a decision when you are passionate, tired, sick, or discouraged.

- **Let God speak to you in the midst of the decision.**
  Create a spiritual environment that is conducive to hearing God. Stay in His presence. Read the Scriptures and ask Father to speak to you. Pursue wise counsel from people who know God's Word and who love you.

- **Determine that you are going to make the right choice, even when circumstances or people are pushing you to do the easy thing.**
  Right choices often cost more in time, money, and effort. Doing the right thing now can save great heartache later.

- **Learn from your mistakes.**
  When you fail, don't think of yourself as a failure. Remember that failure is never final. It can be the pathway for gaining greater wisdom. Your failures are simply the tuition you are paying to learn what doesn't work. Forgive yourself quickly. Pick yourself up and try again, this time with God's grace and guidance. You don't have to go it alone. All of us need help from God and others. Pride keeps you from getting the help you need. Get humble and stretch out a hand to your Father and to others willing to help you.

You can't worship at somebody else's altar. You may bask in the light of another person's glory for a while but you will find that it is a fleeting glory. You might even have an experience with God in another person's vineyard. But, vicarious worship cannot see you through. Serving God through another will not last forever. There can be no substitution for your Savior, no bartering for spiritual experiences, and no shortcuts to the finish line. You will have to travel your own journey and make sacrifices at the altar you have built.

—Bill Wilson

Life is a process of becoming, a combination of states we have to go through. Where people fail is that they wish to elect a state and remain in it. This is a kind of death.

When we blindly adopt a religion, a political system, a literary dogma, we become automatons. We cease to grow.

—Anais Nin

...The credit belongs to the man who is actually in the arena, whose face is marred by dust and sweat and blood, who strives valiantly, who errs and comes short again and again, who knows the great enthusiasms, the great devotions, and spends himself in a worthy cause, who at best knows achievement and who at the worst if he fails at least fails while daring greatly so that his place shall never be with those cold and timid souls who know neither victory nor defeat.

—Theodore Roosevelt

CHAPTER 10

YOU HAVE TO BUILD YOUR OWN ALTAR

So the Reubenites, the Gadites and the half-tribe of Manasseh
left the Israelites at Shiloh in Canaan to return to Gilead, their
own land, which they had acquired in accordance with the
command of the Lord through Moses.

When they came to Geliloth near the Jordan in the land of
Canaan, the Reubenites, the Gadites and the half-tribe of Man-
asseh built an imposing altar there by the Jordan. And when
the Israelites heard that they had built the altar on the border
of Canaan at Geliloth near the Jordan on the Israelite side, the
whole assembly of Israel gathered at Shiloh to go to war
against them...

"If we have built our own altar to turn away from the Lord
and to offer burnt offerings and grain offerings, or to sacri-
fice fellowship offerings on it, may the Lord Himself call us
to account.

"No! We did it for fear that some day your descendants might
say to ours, 'What do you have to do with the Lord, the God of
Israel? The Lord has made the Jordan a boundary between us
and you—you Reubenites and Gadites! You have no share in
the Lord.' So your descendants might cause ours to stop fear-
ing the Lord.

"That is why we said, 'Let us get ready and build an altar—
but not for burnt offerings or sacrifices.' On the contrary, it is
to be a witness between us and you and the generations that
follow, that we will worship the Lord at His sanctuary with
our burnt offerings, sacrifices and fellowship offerings. Then
in the future your descendants will not be able to say to ours,
'You have no share in the Lord'" (Josh. 22:9-12;23-27, NIV).

As Israel's twelve tribes were preparing to enter the Promised Land, a conflict arose. Most of the tribes had planned to settle on the western side of the Jordan, but the tribes of Reuben, Gad, and the half tribe of Manasseh asked Moses if they could settle on the eastern side. It seemed like no big deal, so Moses gave the okay. Moses explained that if they would fight the last battle with the other tribes, and if Israel prevailed, then they could settle on the eastern side.

Israel won the battle and now the land was in the process of being allocated to the various tribes. The two and a half tribes then moved to the eastern side, but here's the principle—don't miss it. The two and a half tribes did something very unusual; they built an altar on the eastern side of the Jordan. That may not sound like a big deal to some of you, but if you know Hebrew history, you'll know that there was only one altar. There was only one altar, and it was at that place where Israel worshiped and the sacrifices were made. When word got back to the other tribes on the western side, they were furious. This act was so offensive to them that they actually planned to wage war and kill the two and a half tribes.

The tribes on the West Bank sent a group of emissaries over to try and clear things up. Upon meeting with the other tribes, they determined that their motives were pure. They learned that the people would still come over to be with the rest of Israel for the feasts and for sacrifices to be offered on the altar located with the Tabernacle.

The delegation then asked why another altar was built on the other side of the Jordan. They were told that the altar was built as a witness to their unity with all of Israel, not for the purpose of sacrifices. They did not want the Jordan River to be a future obstacle that would create division. This altar would be a sign that they were Israelites and committed to the God of Israel.

HAVE YOU BUILT AN ALTAR?

I decided to visit St. Petersburg, Florida and once again see the place where my mother abandoned me on the street corner so many years ago. As I entered the area, many memories rushed into my conscious thoughts. I remembered that the man who picked me up was a Christian. Since I had no place to live, I ended up living in a church closet. The women of the church would rotate, so that each night someone different would bring me a plate of food.

I was just a kid, so they would put a plate of food in front of the closet door on the floor, and then knock on the door. Then I would come out, sit on the floor, and eat. When I was done, I would go back in, do my homework, go to sleep, and then get up for school the next day. I lived that monotonous routine for many years.

I wanted to see that old church building, and I remember being pretty excited. It would be kind of nice to go back and see where I came from. Driving in the rental car down 16th Street, I finally pulled into the parking lot of what used to be the old First Assembly of God church. I was shocked. Where was the building? The building was gone; it had been torn down.

Then, I decided to find one of my old youth pastors. He was the one that taught me how to win souls. When I was in the youth group, they would take us out and teach us how to hand out gospel tracts. I was shy because I had never been around people too much. So, I was never able to just hand a tract to someone. What I would do is put them in phone booths, and then stand across the street and just watch. I remember the first time somebody went in, picked up the tract, and put it in their pocket. I remember it just like it was yesterday, and that was a long time ago. I was stunned to find out that my old youth director was in prison for attempted murder.

When I was in the latter years of high school and getting ready to go into Bible school, my home pastor took care of me. He saw something in me that nobody else saw. Those who have seen me will notice that I sometimes favor my right foot. It's deformed because I never had new shoes when I was little. Therefore, my right foot didn't grow properly. I also have a deformity in my rib cage formed from rickets caused by malnutrition when I was a kid.

I remembered the first new pair of shoes I ever owned, my home pastor had bought for me. The first suit of clothes I ever owned, he also bought for me. The day he committed suicide was probably the hardest day of my adult life.

They're all gone now. The building is gone, the youth director is gone, and the pastor is gone. When I went to Bible school, we had three presidents in four years. None of them could cut it. That's how I've lived ever since I became a Christian. Everything in my past seems to keep fading away. I can't really anchor myself into my past. It is shifting sand.

So now people ask me how I made it with so many obstacles and disappointments. The answer is easy. I made it because, a long time ago, I built my own altar. I built my own altar just in case. I guess I needed it, didn't I? Those altars are created to remind me how good God has been to me. Times, people, and circumstances might have left deep disappointment, but Father has never disappointed me. That altar is a testimony to His faithfulness.

TRUSTING GOD OR TRUSTING MAN

Many people like to live vicariously through their denomination, or the institutions they serve, or some religious personality. This is very dangerous and such substitute living should be avoided. One day, the institution will be gone or will disappoint you. Not one denomination recorded in church history has remained committed to its original vision for longer than one hundred years. Never has it happened in the history of organized religion, and it never will. Unfortunately, a machine is usually created around the man and his message, and eventually all that is left is a memorial to the man, without the power and passion he possessed.

Don't build an altar to the organization. Organizations can be helpful and, when operated in the proper way, can accomplish much as long as they remain committed to the original vision. However, don't put too much stock in it. Don't put too much faith in any institution, because institutions come and go. Also, be careful how much faith you put in individuals, because they come and go as well. Remember that, first and foremost, your faith and trust must be in God, and then it flows into relationships with others. No relationship should ever supersede your relationship with Father.

The tribes on the eastern side of Jordan understood something important. The altar isn't for the nation or the people. Nations and people come and go. The altar is for God. They weren't putting their trust in human ability to keep the vision strong; they put their trust in God. The altar stood forever as a testimony to God's faithfulness, and their commitment to Him.

Someone may ask me, "What do you believe?" They may be shocked that I don't believe in the church, in the leaders, or in the organization. All of those are important and often necessary. But, there is only one object to my faith—God. I've built an altar in my life to worship Him—not a ministry, not an ideal, not an organization.

Worshiping at False Altars

Some people build an altar to a personality. They worship that personality. They follow that leader wherever he or she goes. But when that person falls, the altar crumbles and the clones that worshiped at a false altar are left devastated and abandoned. Worship God, not people. You would think we would have figured this out by now, but we haven't.

Others build an altar to the past as captured by an institution or organization. They devote their lives to serving the institution or the ministry rather than serving God. But, they discover that such service is empty and unfulfilling. Serve God, not the ministry.

A few decide to build an altar to their own vision. Not even that is enough. Visions change. God is always doing a new thing. Altars attached to past vision can never offer fresh encounters with God. God is moving on. Are you moving with Him? Is your altar to a living God, or a dead idea?

Build Your Own Altar

"So, how have you made it, Bill Wilson?" I'll tell you how I made it. I built an altar to God in my own life. It doesn't matter what institutions do, nor does it matter what individuals do. You see…

> *My hope is built on nothing less*
> *Than Jesus' blood and righteousness.*
> *I dare not trust the sweetest ray,*
> *But only lean on Jesus' name.*
> *On Christ the solid rock I stand,*
> *All other ground is sinking sand.*
> (Edward Mote, William B. Bradbury)

If you're going to make it, if you're going to cross the line, then take hold of this concept. You never know, one day you may be standing in a parking lot all alone, or you may be standing in a courtroom like a common criminal, and everybody that said they would stay with you, abandoned you. Then, you stand alone. Never forget that, when others fail you, He will never fail you. You can stand if you have your feet on the sure foundation of a commitment to Christ.

You can't worship at somebody else's altar. You may bask in the light of another person's glory for a while, but you will find that it is a fleeting glory. You might even have an experience with God in another person's vineyard. But, vicarious worship cannot see you through. Serving God through another will not last forever. There can be no substitution for your Savior, no bartering for spiritual experiences, and no shortcuts to the finish line. You will have to travel your own journey and make sacrifices at the altar you have built. The One who has brought you out from bondage and sin and into His vision for your life is the One who will see you through. Nobody else can do that. Build your own altar to God.

LIFE PRINCIPLES IN THE CROSSHAIRS:

- **Don't depend on altars that cannot last.**
  One irrational belief that Albert Ellis suggested was, "I need to depend on something or someone stronger than myself." All human beings and institutions come and go. I understand that we need people but, in the end, you must place your supreme trust in God. He is the only One to whom you need to build an altar.

- **Build your own altar.**
  No one else can build it for you, and you cannot worship forever at an altar someone else has built. The altar that's still standing when all others fall is the one that you have built with faith in Christ.

- **Stand firm.**
  Others may abandon their altars. Others may criticize your altar. But God has given you a vision, a purpose, a direction, and an open door through which you enter into your ministry. What you do doesn't depend on anyone's altar except your own. Built it. Maintain it. Worship God there and stand firm. Paul writes, "Watch, stand fast in the faith, be brave, be strong" (1 Cor. 16:13, NKJV). That's what you do when you build your own altar to God.

PART 3

Principles of
Maintaining Your Focus

Someone once said that if you try to sit on two stools you would eventually fall to the ground. Focus is a major key to discovering solutions to problems and peeking into the future for new possibilities.

Ralph Waldo Emerson said that concentration is the secret of strength in politics, in war, in trade—in all management of human affairs. In this section, we will examine the lives of some godly, and not so godly, men who will teach us lessons on the power of focus.

When faced with an obstacle, Jonathan will show us how to survive when you find yourself between a rock and a hard place. King Rehoboam will teach you the danger of not keeping up your guard when the enemy is attacking you. Peter will show you the danger of focusing on the secondary and losing sight of what is primary. Hezekiah will explain the horror when your personal life gets exposed and finally, Jephthah will demonstrate the price one pays when making and keeping a commitment.

On the way through the real battles in life, you will en-counter a series of little skirmishes that you must fight through. People often pray that God will give them strength for the battle. That's not how it works. **You don't get strength _for_ a battle; you get strength _from_ the battle.**
—Bill Wilson

All endeavor calls for the ability to tramp the last mile, shape the last plan, endure the last hour's toil. The fight to the finish spirit is the one...characteristic we must posses if we are to face the future as finishers.
—Author Unknown

Do you not know that those who run in a race all run, but only one receives the prize? Run in such a way that you may win.
—Apostle Paul

CHAPTER 11

BETWEEN A ROCK
AND A HARD PLACE

RETREATING FROM YOUR TROUBLES OR GOING THROUGH YOUR TROUBLES

What do you do when you find yourself between a rock and a hard place? We have all been at that place many times during our lives. Many people simply stop. They give up and refuse to move forward. They put the vision on hold and eventually lose all heart. Over the last thirty-five years of ministry, I have seen pastors, Sunday school teachers, church leaders, and entire churches come to a grinding halt and sadly, they are never able to overcome the circumstance pressing in on them. The result is that they never will accomplish anything else in God's kingdom. Why? They thought that they were facing a mountain too formidable to climb. They were between a rock and a hard place. They could not find the wisdom or the courage to press over the obstacles that stood in their way. Their problems became a wall rather than a way into new opportunities for spiritual reality. They were seeking for an *exit* out of their troubles rather than seeing their problems as an *entry* into new opportunities. When they stopped, they fizzled out and never again had an impact in their community just because they ran up against an obstacle, some sort of a situation or problem, and were not able to go beyond it.

I've seen churches split right down the middle and watched close friends become enemies because something happens that seems impossible to overcome. A problem arises or a situation occurs and people don't know what to do. Therefore, they allow their emotions, feelings, frustration, and anxiety to drive them. However, the issue is not so much what happens to you, as it is how you respond to what happens. When you encounter difficulties, you must learn not to react but to respond. If you recoil in fear and discouragement, you have lost the battle. But if you respond with faith and courage, you will find a way through your mountain of trouble.

Read how Jonathan, Saul's son, provides an example for us to follow:

> One day Jonathan son of Saul said to the young man bearing his armor, "Come, let's go over to the Philistine outpost on the other side." But he did not tell his father.
>
> Saul was staying on the outskirts of Gibeah under a pomegranate tree in Migron. With him were about six hundred men, among whom was Ahijah, who was wearing an ephod. He was a son of Ichabod's brother Ahitub son of Phinehas, the son of Eli, the Lord's priest in Shiloh. No one was aware that Jonathan had left.
>
> On each side of the pass that Jonathan intended to cross to reach the Philistine outpost was a cliff; one was called Bozez, and the other Seneh. One cliff stood to the north toward Micmash, the other to the south toward Geba.
>
> Jonathan said to his young armor-bearer, "Come, let's go over to the outpost of those uncircumcised fellows. Perhaps the Lord will act in our behalf. Nothing can hinder the Lord from saving, whether by many or by few."
>
> "Do all that you have in mind," his armor-bearer said. "Go ahead; I am with you heart and soul."
>
> Jonathan said, "Come, then; we will cross over toward the men and let them see us. If they say to us, 'Wait there until we come to you,' we will stay where we are and not go up to them. But if they say, 'Come up to us,' we will climb up, because that will be our sign that the Lord has given them into our hands."
>
> So both of them showed themselves to the Philistine outpost. "Look!" said the Philistines. "The Hebrews are crawling out of the holes they were hiding in." The men of the outpost shouted to Jonathan and his armor-bearer, "Come up to us and we'll teach you a lesson."
>
> So Jonathan said to his armor-bearer, "Climb up after me; the Lord has given them into the hand of Israel" (1 Sam. 14:1-12, NIV).

Jonathan saw this Philistine outpost as a threat to Israel and wanted to take it out. He enlisted his faithful armor-bearer to join him in the battle. As they approached the pass, they saw that two massive cliffs hedged in the pass, and both men literally found themselves between a rock and a hard place. They were trying to cross between these two ranges and, quite frankly, were concerned as to whether they could succeed. Jonathan then laid out the plan and, based upon the Philistines' response, he would know whether God was with them. Once they were assured of God's presence and protection, they proceeded and overcame the Philistines.

When you find yourself trapped between a rock and a hard place, the issue isn't how tough or difficult your circumstance is. The real issue is this: Will you focus on the problem or on the Presence of the One who will help you overcome? The more you focus on being trapped and stuck, the more likely it will be that you will stay trapped and stuck. Studying and analyzing your situation doesn't get you through; it only confirms why you're trapped.

I know many people who can explain to me in intricate detail why they are stuck in the mess they are in. They can't see beyond their present problem to God's possibilities. Their focus is on where they *are* instead of where they're *going*.

STRENGTH COMES FROM THE FIGHT, NOT THE FLIGHT

As you journey through life, you *will* encounter trials and battles through which you must fight. People often pray that God will give them strength for the battle. That's not how it works. You don't get strength *for* a battle; you get strength *from* the battle.

Actually, most Christians desire to run from the battle, but experience proves that you get power in the middle of the fight, not in the flight from the fight. Fleeing battles never won any war. Most Christians feel overwhelmed and ill prepared to fight the battle. So they pray, "O God, spare me from the conflict." They fear getting bruised and battered in the fight. However, the only way to build strength and courage is to go into battle.

Remember Joshua and the Israelites? At first glance, going into the Promised Land looked intimidating. Ten spies reported that there were giants in the land and they felt like grasshoppers compared to the enemy (see Num. 13). So, they ran from the battle. For 40 years, Israel wandered in the wilderness. The original generation of slaves that had left Egypt couldn't face the battles necessary to conquer the Promised Land. They all died before

Israel, led by Joshua, finally crossed the Jordan into the Promised Land.

Be Strong and Very Courageous

What did God say to them? "Be strong and very courageous" (Josh. 1:7a, NIV). Why? Receiving what God has promised isn't easy. It's not a cakewalk. We want God's best, but we want it handed to us on a silver platter. Sorry, it doesn't happen that way. The first thing that Israel faced in the Promised Land wasn't a party; it was a battle. As they fought their way into God's promises, they acquired both strength and courage to continue. You don't get strength *for* a battle; you get strength *from* the battle.

This principle can also be illustrated by the story of David and Goliath. When Saul questioned David about his ability to fight Goliath, David said that he had fought a lion and a bear, and won both times. There was nothing unusual about the story of David and Goliath. In fact, it wasn't a miracle at all. David already had battle experience; he had already gained strength and courage *from the battles* he had fought. He wasn't walking into battle cold and inexperienced, like some people have preached.

I worked with a man named Tommy Barnett for several years. The work we were involved with in Iowa became the fastest growing church in America at that time. Tommy then went to Phoenix, and the church grew explosively. Among the many ministries provided is a wheelchair ministry. They have several buses designed for handicapped people that they used for picking up people who were confined to wheelchairs. One day, a man ran a stop sign and hit the bus, flipping it over. Several of the handicapped people were killed.

Though the church was doing quite well, when the bus overturned and people were killed, the media went ballistic. This was a very discouraging time. They saw their church's name and pastor's face plastered on every newspaper and TV news show. Even in the midst of all the great things that were happening, Pastor Barnett found himself between a rock and a hard place. He didn't quit. He kept going. He had strength and courage from the previous battles he had fought. He had learned this lesson years ago.

Dr. Robert Schuller was in Europe several years ago and was hit in the head with a car door. It was a very difficult time for him, because he was very close to death. He didn't quit. His previous battles had given him the strength and courage to go on and push through his mountain.

Billy Graham, one of the most influential men of modern history, suffers from Parkinson's disease. Yes, he's getting along in years, but that's not what has slowed him down. His faith in God and his willingness to press on and not quit shines as a beacon of strength and hope in the murky darkness of this world. He hasn't quit. He has strength, courage, and endurance to run the race and finish strong.

Most of the great men and women of faith have found themselves between a rock and a hard place at various times in their ministries; it's part of leadership. It's part of stepping out of the box and doing something unusual. If you choose to be a person who chases hard after God, at some point you will find yourself in a position that may not be very pleasant.

So what do you do when you find yourself in a place where you don't really know what to do or how to respond? How is it that some people make it through those places and others don't? Why do they fall apart, or quit? Let's return to Jonathan and his armor-bearer to discover how to gain strength from the battle and get beyond a rock and a hard place.

Five Observations of Overcoming

Observation # 1: Keep on going.

First Samuel 14:4 reports that Jonathan "sought to go over" (NKJV). In other words, he decided to keep moving. This is a vital key to success; a decision must be made. I've often wondered why I'm still in the race when other friends around me have dropped out. Many of them were more talented and gifted than I am. They often had greater vision and bigger dreams. They seemed to be more spiritual and have greater wisdom. The only difference between others that could have gone on and me is that when they come to a rock and a hard place, they stop. I keep on going.

The beauty about Metro Ministries in New York is that it's not built on talent or ability; it's built on *longevity*, and anybody can do that! Not everyone can play the guitar or sing, but one thing everyone can do is keep on going. The marathon isn't completed by how fast a runner leaves the blocks. It isn't won by reputation or previous awards. It's only won by constant commitment to the race over a very long period of time! When your lungs feel like they are going to explode, keep on running. When your legs feel like jelly, keep on running.

Today, we live in a "fast-food" world. We think everything should be in our hands and out the door in less than five minutes. This "fast-food" mentality has created great problems in our culture and in the church as well. We think that success should come easily, without failure and setbacks. We're surrounded by people who quit before they give their efforts a chance to produce. As soon as it gets tough or something bad happens, people want to quit. It is clear that these people do not understand some of the basic philosophies of our Lord. Remember, He said, "...unless a grain of wheat falls into the earth and dies, it remains alone; but if it dies, it bears much fruit" (John 12:24, NASB).

Let me put forth a word that will radically alter how you face problems: *endurance*. Let me add to that: *persistence*. Then, I will finish the thought with: *patience*. Paul says it this way,

> *We can rejoice, too, when we run into problems and trials, for we know that they are good for us—they help us learn to endure. And endurance develops strength of character in us, and character strengthens our confident expectation of salvation. And this expectation will not disappoint us. For we know how dearly God loves us, because he has given us the Holy Spirit to fill our hearts with his love* (Rom. 5:3-5, NLT).

Endurance, persistence, and patience—these are all key qualities that are found in every successful man or woman.

Observation # 2: Encourage someone else to keep going on.

First Jonathan said that he was "going over," but then he said, "*Let us* go over." He encouraged somebody else to keep going. Encourage somebody else to keep going. Let me ask you:

- Do you want to keep going?
- Do you want to stay until the finish?
- Do you want to see the scenery at the end of the journey?

One of the best ways to push through is to encourage someone else to keep going. I can't tell you how many staff meetings I've walked into in New York City, wondering if I could keep going. I was in the battle and was struggling, whether it was financial problems, personal problems, or issues in the ministry. I've witnessed twenty-two murders during my time in New York. We've had staff members raped and killed. I've been stabbed twice. I've had two concussions and I have been shot, point-blank, in the face. This is part of living where I live; it goes with the territory. That's why there are not many people lining up, waiting to live here.

I've often walked in on Friday morning to talk to the staff and it took everything I had to muster up enough energy to get out there and face them. But, I had to do it. My job as the leader is to encourage them to keep going. Encouragement is what leadership is all about. So, as I encourage them and tell them to keep going, I am encouraged. You receive what you sow.

A preacher told me, not too long ago, that he had followed what I was doing for 25 years. He said he couldn't believe I'm still going. But, you see, I chose not to quit. Did you catch it? I *chose* not to quit. It's a choice. That preacher told me that if I can do it, he could do it. Bingo! That's the response. If I can do it, you can do it. Paul wrote,

> So encourage each other and build each other up, just as you are already doing. Dear brothers and sisters, honor those who are your leaders in the Lord's work. They work hard among you and warn you against all that is wrong. Think highly of them and give them your wholehearted love because of their work. And remember to live peaceably with each other. Brothers and sisters, we urge you to warn those who are lazy. Encourage those who are timid. Take tender care of those who are weak. Be patient with everyone (1 Thess. 5:11-14, NLT).

Observation #3: You will pass over.

Jonathan didn't say, "I *think* we're going to pass over." He said, "We *will* pass over." I knew an old missionary years ago, and his favorite saying was, "We're going to make it. We may not look like much when we get there, but we're going to make it." I like that. We're going to make it! "The tongue has the power of life and death, and those who love it will eat its fruit" (Prov. 18:21, NIV). I hope that you take hold of this truth and let it seep into your being. You speak, and things happen. You have the power of life and death in your tongue, so how do you speak to each other? If you live in the world of negative thought, that is the world that you will create around you. If you speak positively, you will draw people to you and create a positive environment around you. Your tongue creates the world you live in.

Several years ago, I was ministering at a church in Orlando. Between the first and second Sunday morning services, I received a call from New York saying that my mother had been found dead in the street. I was in the office with the pastor and the pastor's secretary. The type of conversation I was having on the phone was obvious to them, so, when I hung up, the pastor asked what had happened. I told him, and he asked if I was able to preach the second service. I told him, "Yes." The church secretary looked at me and said, "You're like a machine, aren't you?" No, I'm not a machine. However, when I make a commitment to do something, I do it. Feelings or emotions don't distract me; I just do it. That is how you survive, ministering for thirty-five years. Don't fly by the seat of your pants as a leader. If you do, you're in the wrong business.

Before the battle, during the battle, and after the victory, I know that feelings and emotions haven't seen me through. I have the faith of God and the confident expectation that I will make it. I'm not arrogant or proud. I just know two things: God is faithful and I have decided to be faithful to Him.

Some people say, "God is faithful." Then they just sit around and wait for God to do a miracle and get them beyond a rock and a hard place. But the living God, who is faithful, dwells in me. He has deposited in me His Spirit who gives me the confidence to get up and go on. Jesus commends the "good and faithful" servant (Mt. 25:21). Why? That servant took what the master had faithfully entrusted to him and did something with it! I am committed to using what God has faithfully given me to push through my rock and hard places. What about you?

Observation # 4: Announce that you are going on!

Make the announcement. Put it on the Internet and broadcast it to everyone. Put it in the book. "How can I be sure that I can keep going on?" you ask. *You've got a living God.*

When I first went to New York, everybody said it couldn't be done because it had never been done. What has happened in Metro Ministries in New York City has never been done, ever, in the history of the United States of America. So, naturally, a person who pioneers something that has not been done pays the price. Pioneers got shot at by both the cowboys and the Indians. The first guy up front is the one that catches all the shots. The ones that follow him have a little bit easier time. The nature of the pioneer is to create a pathway for others to follow.

Babe Ruth, of the old New York Yankees, would take the baseball bat and point to where he was going to hit the home run. I like someone who is that positive and confident in the face of the opposing team to say, "Hey! I'm hitting it right over there, and there isn't anything you can do about it."

I want you to get that kind of spirit. "I'm going right over there, right now, and there is nothing you can do about it. You can try, but you aren't going to do it." That, my friend, is what we're talking about here.

Too many people don't go on because they don't have a clear vision of where they are going. When God has set the vision in front of you, announce it, write it down, live it out. The living God, who gave you that vision, goal, and dream, has already been where you are going. He's the Alpha and the Omega. He has prepared a place for you to step into; you're walking forward into His destiny for you. Only the ones with a clear vision are able to move forward through adversity and opposition. Jesus' determination was described this way by the writer of Hebrews, "... fixing our eyes on Jesus, the author and perfecter of faith, who for the joy set before Him endured the cross, despising the shame, and has sat down at the right hand of the throne of God" (Heb. 12:2, NASB). His eyes were filled with the objective set before Him, not the opposition set against Him.

Tell everyone about where the living God is leading you. Don't give yourself an out. Say what you mean and then act on it. James writes that faith without works is dead (see James 2:17). Speak it and then act!

Observation # 5: Follow me!

Jonathan looked at his armor bearer and said, "Come up after me." Jonathan went first. It's hard to tell others to keep going if you're not going yourself. Somebody has to step out first and lead. Someone has to say, "Follow me, I'll do it first. If I can do it, you can do it, too."

C.M. Ward was an old-time Pentecostal preacher who used to say something that I thought was very funny. He said, even if you get run out of town, get out front and make everybody else think it's a parade. I like that; it makes sense to me. Get out front! If you're going to lead, take the reins, take the bull by the horns, get out front and lead. Like someone once said, "Lead, follow, or get out of the way!"

Jonathan and his armor bearer came to a certain place on their way to the battle. They weren't actually there yet—they were on the way. Sometimes, you think you're in the battle, but you aren't. You're just on the way.

I was looking through a replica of Christopher Columbus' diary and noticed that there were times that he was in danger of being thrown overboard by his own people. His crew thought he was a nut and that they were all going to die with him. Things got so bad that they were prepared to throw him overboard and turn back. Nevertheless, every night when Columbus wrote in his diary, the last thing he wrote at the end of every entry was, "…and this day we sailed on." What did he do? He just kept on going.

That is your charge as well. When things get so tough you can barely stand, keep pressing on. Follow the last command. Keep going. Paul wrote, "Brothers, I do not consider myself yet to have taken hold of it. But one thing I do: Forgetting what is behind and straining toward what is ahead, I press on toward the goal to win the prize for which God has called me heavenward in Christ Jesus" (Phil. 3:13-14, NIV).

LIFE PRINCIPLES IN THE CROSSHAIRS:

- **You don't get strength *for* a battle; you get strength *from* the battle.**
- **Don't quit…keep on going.**
- **Encourage someone else to keep on going.**
- **You will pass over.**
- **Announce to others that you are going on.**
- **Be a leader. Invite others to follow you.**

Don't lose the gold. People lose the gold because they don't really know what they have. They fail to realize the real treasures and gifts that God has placed in their hands. They do not understand that they are responsible for the gift of life that has been given to them.

—Bill Wilson

Action springs not from thought, but from a readiness for responsibility.

—Dietrich Bonhoeffer

You can't escape the responsibility of tomorrow by evading it today.

—Abraham Lincoln

I believe that every right implies a responsibility; every opportunity, an obligation; every possession, a duty.

—John D. Rockefeller, Jr.

CHAPTER 12

DO YOUR OWN GUARD DUTY

In the fifth year of King Rehoboam, Shishak king of Egypt at-
tacked Jerusalem. He carried off the treasures of the temple of
the Lord and the treasures of the royal palace. He took every-
thing, including all the gold shields Solomon had made. So
King Rehoboam made bronze shields to replace them and as-
signed these to the commanders of the guard on duty at the en-
trance to the royal palace. Whenever the king went to the
Lord's temple, the guards bore the shields, and afterward they
returned them to the guardroom (1 Kings 14:25-28, NIV).

King Rehoboam made a terrible mistake. In his fifth year of
his reign as king over Judah, the king of Egypt came up against
Judah and pillaged the city of Jerusalem. During the battle,
Shishak, king of Egypt, invaded the Jewish temple and took,
among many precious temple assets, the shields of gold made by
Solomon that were kept in the temple. As I contemplated this story,
I had several questions that bothered me and were begging for an
answer:

- How could you possibly allow an enemy to come in
  and steal something so valuable?

- Why was no guard posted?

- Did Rehoboam understand the true value of what
  had been lost?

Rehoboam did not honor the throne like his grandfather,
David, nor did he honor the people like his father, Solomon. He
was self-centered, cruel, and sought only to accumulate wealth for
himself rather than distribute to the needs of others. The wealth
that Solomon had amassed during his reign was unequalled to
that of any other ruler in the world. Unfortunately, even though
Rehoboam inherited much wealth, he was a pauper in his heart.
He didn't have a clue about the value of wealth and what could

be accomplished through these riches. If you don't understand the value of what you have you will eventually lose it, as Rehoboam did.

Because of his self-serving ways, the king gave no thought to the adequate protection of the temple of God and what was inside. The rich treasures of Judah were kept in the temple, but Rehoboam had no appreciation for their ancient significance and precious worth. Why then did Rehoboam dishonor the national treasure? Why was the temple left unguarded? We can't answer all of these questions, but certainly there are some valuable observations that we can learn from this historical event.

Observation # 1: Don't lose the gold in the first place.

Don't lose the gold. People lose the gold because they don't really know what they have. They fail to realize the real treasures and gifts that God has placed in their hands. They do not understand that they are responsible for the gift of life that has been given to them. Sometimes, we fail to consider the past and be thankful for how far God has brought us.

Why do I still live in a warehouse in Brooklyn, New York? Why do I still drive the bus? Why do I eat dinner with homeless people? *Because I never want to forget where I came from.* Often, when we begin to experience success, we slowly commence to drift further away from our origins and, at the same time, we forget what God has done in our lives. As we lose touch with our beginnings we also lose the passion that spiritually drove us in those days.

I've watched this sad phenomenon occur over and over again in the Church. There is a time when you are so passionate about ministering to the ones who are still in the place from where you have come. The power of your testimony was so vivid and compelling that you are often reaching out to others, hoping to bring them into the Kingdom. Your experience with Christ was so real, and you talked to Him every day. You loved the Scriptures and were reading and memorizing them all the time. God was speaking to you and it was so powerful. You also were involved in your church and were surrounded by a wonderful pastor and loving friends. But as the weeks, months, and years rolled along, you began to take these things for granted. Life began to drain your spiritual energy. You no longer speak of what God has done in your life. The fire of passion has been consumed by your own selfish desires. You've grown tired of reading the Scriptures and the words of the Lord are no longer ringing in your ears. Once it is all gone, you begin to realize what you really had. You never realized what you had until it's been taken away by satan, the great gold-robber. How many well-known preachers have we watched, slowly but surely, stop doing the very hands-on ministry that brought them to a level of notoriety in the first place?

How could you lose something this valuable? It might be a good idea to take inventory and begin to recognize what you have and what you might have lost. Rehoboam didn't have a clue about what he had and, because he had no concept of its precious value, it was easy for him to justify his losses. We need to value our spiritual heritage and the things Father has given us. Don't lose the gold!

Observation # 2: If it gets stolen, replace it.

It if gets stolen, replace it as quickly as you can. Watch how Rehoboam seeks to cover up what he has lost. He replaced them with brass shields. Gold is symbolic of God, while brass is symbolic of man. Rehoboam replaced his godly wealth with fleshly wealth. How often does this happen? When we lose our connection to heaven, we are tempted to replace it with our own human resources. Rather than depending on the gifts God has given us, we so easily replace them with our own human abilities. They did this because they could never afford to build the gold ones again.

Don't lose the gold. If you lose the shields, you can try to replace them, but it will be very hard to replace the gold again. Once you lose it, it will be a challenge to get back what you had before. If you lose the gold in your life, that is, if you have a great personal failure, then it is very possible that you will have a limp like Jacob for the rest of your life. It will not disqualify you from ministry, but it will make it difficult to overcome those "watchdogs" in the Church who are always ready to criticize and condemn those who have fallen. "Ho! Everyone who thirsts, come to the waters; and you who have no money come, buy and eat. Yes, come, buy wine and milk without money and without price" (Isa. 55:1, NKJV). If you should lose your gold, the prophet Isaiah has excellent counsel for you. If you ever get your spiritual hunger back, then that hunger will give you the down payment you need to get the gold back into your life.

Rehoboam didn't understand this principle. After the tribute he had to pay the king of Egypt, his treasury was too small to replace the golden shields. An important inheritance was lost that day, and you can't replace inheritance. You may be able to replace the things, but not the inheritance.

Don't lose what you have. Don't trade the proverbial birthright for the bowl of soup, because you will regret it for the rest of your life. Something that has always bothered me in certain churches is their Sunday night "come up to the altar and get right" service. Many went to the altar, confessed sin, but never repented. To repent is to turn away from sin and to do what's right.

When you confess, repent and get it right. Make a *decision* to get right. Many people want the relief of confession, but are unwilling to pay the price of repentance—turning away from sin and doing what's right.

If you are young, make your decisions wisely. Coming to an altar at church and shedding a few tears will get your sins forgiven and you'll go to heaven, but you'll live in hell in this life. You can really have it any way you want. See, God really only gives us two choices in life: obey or disobey. Either we do it His way or we don't. Let's cut to the chase: God gave you a brain for a reason. You can use it or lose it, make it or break it. I've seen enough hell on this earth, and lived through some of it, that I don't want to spend eternity there.

Some say not to scare others with hell, or else their decisions won't last. Well, if it lasts for a while and they get to know God and then turn their backs, they will have their own reward. Use your head. That's why God gave it to you.

Observation # 3: Don't deceive yourself into thinking the brass is gold, because it isn't.

Don't deceive yourself into thinking that the gold is brass just because you tried to replace the gold with brass. Deception is a dangerous, slippery slope to start walking down. If it's brass, it's brass, and that's it. It may be functional as a weapon, but it's still brass and that's all. Therefore, don't kid yourself; it will never be gold. You can never substitute the gift and presence of God in your life with brassy replacements of your own natural abilities and ingenuity.

Several years ago, Steve Martin starred in a movie called *The Lonely Guy*. He played a single man who was lonesome and craving companionship. He visited a therapist who suggested he use cutouts of human forms to give the impression there were guests in his house for a party. It gave the illusion that his house was full of people. But that was all it was—an illusion. The illusion of having people around him did not cure his loneliness. You can never replace the real thing with a replica and think that it will satisfy you and others.

When the Egyptian king took the shields, Israel lost more than just the value of the gold in those shields. The entire temple was desecrated and devalued by the entrance of these foreigners into the sacred places of worship. The shields were memorials, reminding Israel of the glory days of Solomon. They were national treasures that had great emotional value to the people. How would you feel if someone defaced Mt. Rushmore or stole the Liberty Bell? You would feel dishonored and disheartened. To avoid this national shame, the king tried to replace the gold shields with clever reproductions. Substitutions just do not work.

Observation # 4: It takes losing the gold to appreciate the brass.

Often, you must lose the gold to appreciate what you really had. The story has an unusual ending to it. After they reconstructed the shields using brass and put them back in the temple, they assigned guards. Now, that's a Christian deal if I ever saw one. Let's wait until it's all gone and then we're going to guard it. It is quite sad to see how much of Christianity seems to place more value on protecting the veneer of a religious system that is only a semblance of its original power and presence in the world.

If you had guarded it in the first place, you'd still have it. Rather than protecting our self-made religious constructions, we should be trying to figure out how we can get back the original essence of who we are as God's people.

Many people in ministry who are older than I often regret their mistakes and wish they could do parts of their ministry over again. History repeats itself because we're too stupid to learn the first time. Israel wandered in the desert for forty years because they could never get on with the plan of God.

Every one of us has to do his own guard duty. Don't depend on somebody else to do it for you, because they aren't going to do it. I learned that a long time ago. I thought people were guarding it for me. Guess what? They weren't. So now, I do my own guarding, and if I'd been all that bright, I guess I'd have been doing my own in the first place. No one can walk the journey for you. No one can protect you from the loss of your spiritual life. You have to walk your own journey. You have to be responsible for what has been given to you.

"For it is just like a man about to go on a journey, who called his own slaves, and entrusted his possessions to them" (Matt. 25:14, NASB). Like the servants in the story of the talents, we have been entrusted with heavenly treasure, and Father is looking to see how we will be responsible for what has been given to us. Will you guard carefully what has been given to you?

The solid gold at the center of your life that needs guarding is your heart. Once that's guarded, you will be able to guard the other relationships in life that are important to God and you. Here's how to guard your gold, your heart:

Above all else, guard your heart, for it affects everything you do. Avoid all perverse talk; stay far from corrupt speech. Look straight ahead, and fix your eyes on what lies before you. Mark out a straight path for your feet; then stick to the path and stay safe. Don't get sidetracked; keep your feet from following evil (Prov. 4:23-27, NLT).

LIFE PRINCIPLES IN THE CROSSHAIRS:

- **Don't lose the gold that God has entrusted to you.**

- **If it gets stolen, replace it quickly.**

- **Don't deceive yourself into thinking that brass is gold. Replace gold with gold. Imitations and substitutions do not work in God's kingdom.**

- **It takes losing the precious gold to help you appreciate what you have had.**

As leaders, there are many things that compete for our affection, creating diversions that can sidetrack us from our mission. Such intrusions become distractions in our relationship with Christ, our relationships with others with whom and to whom we minister, and in our ministry effectiveness.

—Bill Wilson

Modern civilization is so complex as to make the devotional life all but impossible. It wears us out by multiplying distractions and beats us down, destroying our solitude, where otherwise we might drink and renew our strength, before going out to face the world again. "Commune with your own heart upon your bed and be still," is a wise and healing counsel; but how can it be followed in this day of the newspaper, the telephone, the radio and television? These modern playthings, like pet tiger cubs, have grown so large and dangerous that they threaten to devour us all...The need for solitude and quietness was never greater than it is today.

—A. W. Tozer

Nothing of value is ever acquired without discipline... ["the spiritual masters of days gone by"] *have warned us that the one who would get in touch with the soul must do so with diligence and determination. One must overcome feelings, fatigue, distractions, errant appetites, and popular opinion.*

—Gordon MacDonald

CHAPTER 13

DON'T COUNT THE FISH

"I'm going out to fish," Simon Peter told them, and they said, "We'll go with you." So they went out and got into the boat, but that night they caught nothing.

Early in the morning, Jesus stood on the shore, but the disciples did not realize that it was Jesus.

He called out to them, "Friends, haven't you any fish?"

"No," they answered.

He said, "Throw your net on the right side of the boat and you will find some." When they did, they were unable to haul the net in because of the large number of fish.

Then the disciple whom Jesus loved said to Peter, "It is the Lord!" As soon as Simon Peter heard him say, "It is the Lord," he wrapped his outer garment around him (for he had taken it off) and jumped into the water. The other disciples followed in the boat, towing the net full of fish, for they were not far from shore, about a hundred yards. When they landed, they saw a fire of burning coals there with fish on it, and some bread.

Jesus said to them, "Bring some of the fish you have just caught."

Simon Peter climbed aboard and dragged the net ashore. It was full of large fish, 153, but even with so many the net was not torn. Jesus said to them, "Come and have breakfast." None of the disciples dared ask Him, "Who are you?" They knew it was the Lord. Jesus came, took the bread and gave it to them, and did the same with the fish. This was now the third time Jesus appeared to His disciples after He was raised from the dead.

When they had finished eating, Jesus said to Simon Peter, "Simon son of John, do you truly love Me more than these?"

"Yes, Lord," he said, "You know that I love You."

Jesus said, "Feed My lambs."

Again Jesus said, "Simon son of John, do you truly love Me?"
He answered, "Yes, Lord, You know that I love You."
Jesus said, "Take care of My sheep."
The third time He said to him, "Simon son of John, do you love Me?"
Peter was hurt because Jesus asked him the third time, "Do you love Me?" He said, "Lord, You know all things; You know that I love You."
Jesus said, "Feed My sheep" (John 21:3-17, NIV).

LET'S GO FISHING

The disciples had fished all night and caught absolutely nothing. By the early morning hours they were weary and frustrated. Suddenly from the shore they heard a voice yelling out to them. Jesus was waiting for them on the shore, but they didn't recognize that it was Jesus. He called out again and asked if they had caught any fish. Somewhat discouraged they yelled back that they had not caught any fish. Jesus told them to cast their net on the right side. We are often guilty of reading Bible stories rather quickly and thus missing the impact of the events. One can almost feel the agitation in the disciples as Jesus, the carpenter, tells John, Peter and the other fishermen to try the other side of the boat. Well, they probably had been fishing both sides of the boat all night long. Nevertheless, what harm could it do? He was the Master, you know. And as the story goes, they pulled in an abundance of fish, much to their surprise.

When the disciples reached the shore, Jesus has already arranged things so that they could start cooking the fish. He told them to bring all the fish. The Bible states that 153 fish were caught. Now, ask yourself: "How did they know that there were 153 fish?" I think it is obvious. Somebody counted them! Someone counted the fish, and I have a feeling that it was Peter. He was always the one doing impetuous things. Somebody counted the fish and they recorded it, 153 fish. Without a doubt this was probably a record catch.

After they had finished their fried fish on that Galilean shore, they all leaned back and just savored the moment. In that moment of contemplation, Jesus broke the silence by asking Peter, "Do you love Me more than these?" I'm sure that you've heard countless numbers of sermons preached on this subject. Of course, we know that when you look at the Greek text that Jesus was asking Peter about *agape* love, which is unconditional, and Peter's answer was with *philos*, which is the normal, earthly, human love.

MISSING THE OBVIOUS

However, I want you to catch this. If you had been fishing all night and caught nothing, then suddenly you were on the shore with *one* catch of 153 fish (probably your record catch), what would your mind be contemplating? It would be on the 153 fish, wouldn't it? You would be overwhelmed and obsessed with the miracle of that catch. Sure, because that's the human side. We are quicker to observe the obvious as the ambiguous eludes us.

Jesus asked Peter if he loved Him more than he loved "these." What were "these"? Jesus was not talking about the other disciples, the world, or anything else. He was pointing to the fish!

"Peter, do you love Me more than these 153 fish? Do you love Me more than what I just did for you?"

Many of us really like what God can do for us, and it is a challenge not to miss the Giver in the midst of receiving the gifts. As someone once said, "Beggars seek His hands, while lovers seek His face." It is easy to become infatuated with the gifts and lose sight of the Giver. This is a very common mistake for leaders. Jesus asks:

- Do you love Me more than the miracle I've just performed?

- Do you love Me more than a full bus of children coming to Sunday school?

- Do you love Me more than the ministry that you are building?

- Do you love Me more than the miracles that are happening in your life and ministry?

While Jesus is sitting right there in front of him, there's Peter,
"136, 137, 138, 139."
"Hey! Peter!"
"140..."
"Hey! Hey, Peter!"
"146, 147."
"Hey!"

It's easy to get so caught up in *the work of the Lord* and totally forget *the Lord of the work*. Many have done it; I know that I have. Why? Because I like the work. I love doing what I'm doing, driving the Sunday school bus in New York City. It's my favorite thing. Narrow streets, double-parked cars, that's got my name all over it. But all of us must be very careful that we do not allow our work to compete with our affections for the Lord. Besides being good workers in the field, we need to learn how to be lovers in Father's house.

THREE COMPETITORS FOR OUR AFFECTION

As leaders, there are many things that compete for our affection, creating diversions that can sidetrack us from our mission. Such intrusions become distractions in our relationship with Christ, our relationships with others with whom and to whom we minister, and in our ministry effectiveness. There are three dangerous competitors for our affections.

Competitor # 1: Answered prayers compete for our affection.

One sermon I occasionally preach is entitled, "The Danger of Raising $110,000." It springs from an experience we had at Metro in which God moved in a mighty way. We were in danger of losing our first building. To save ourselves from losing this precious piece of property, we gave everything we had. I was doing everything I could to raise money and people were making great sacrifices. Elderly women were even giving their jewelry and watches to sell and raise enough money to keep this building. Despite every effort, we were losing the building, and it was about to be repossessed.

We decided to schedule a "Miracle Sunday" before the deadline, to see if we could raise the final outstanding funds necessary to keep this building. We created a video that other churches could use to show to their congregations the nature of our huge financial needs. Miraculously, in one day, sixteen churches raised $110,000 in cash and paid off the loan for the building.

I had been praying and fasting about raising this money for months, and God answered my prayers! However, after I heard the total of the offering, I was so excited that I actually forgot to thank God. Does that make any sense? Have you ever been there? I was so caught up in the answered prayer that I did the same thing as Peter. I was counting dollars instead of fish, but I was just as distracted as Peter was. My focus was on the gift, not the Giver. I was focused on God's work instead of God Himself. How do we sidestep the competitor for our affection of *answered prayer*? Here are a few suggestions:

- **Listen!** Don't make the focus of your prayers to be striving to get answers to your prayers. True, intimate prayer is a simultaneous process of listening and speaking. Most of the time we get prayer backwards; we talk at God excessively and call it prayer. Prayer is communication, and is best accomplished by listening and sharing from our heartfelt love for Him, not our desire for answers. Make the psalmist's assertions your own, "I listen carefully to what God is saying ..." (see Ps. 85:8). Most of us never get answers to prayers because we don't take time to listen.

- **Obey!** When listening to His voice in prayer, we are not trying to persuade God to do what we want; rather, we are seeking to hear and obey what He wants. When we hear His voice, we only have one option—obey! "No, Lord," is never an option. In fact, it's contradictory. If we say "no," then He's not Lord! "Yes, Lord," is always our only acceptable response. Deuteronomy 15:4-6 reminds us that blessing comes when we "carefully obey the voice of...[our] God" (NKJV).

- **Love!** Make certain that your "first love" is the Lord; a love that is not based on what He does for you. Love Jesus for who He is—your Redeemer, Savior, Friend, and Lover. Remember Jesus' words, "Nevertheless, I have this against you, that you have left your first love" (Rev. 2:4). Jesus spoke that to the believers in the church at Ephesus, who at one time were red-hot in their love for Christ. The believers in that church worked hard for the Lord, but had let their relationship with Him take second place in their lives. Jesus will not share first place with anyone or anything else in your life. His compassion for you will seek to destroy all of those things that will interfere with the passion of a mutual love between the beloved and her Lover.

Competitor # 2: Our own usefulness competes for our affection.

Our own usefulness in the ministry as a leader often competes with our affection for the Lord. I worked with a TV station in the South, trying to get more "Won By One" sponsors signed up. We talked, worked, and planned this event, and finally set a goal of what we wanted to achieve.

Our "work" resulted in four hundred people calling in one night to sponsor a child, the most we've ever had from one television program. We were so excited and were rejoicing over what we had done, and how everybody had done their part.

Later, we, the camera crew, the people doing the backdrops, and my staff, were all sitting around in a restaurant talking, when it hit me again. Everybody had done their part, everybody had worked together, and the night was successful. So, why were we in a restaurant eating dinner, when we all needed to go back, get on our faces and thank God for what He had accomplished? It is so easy for us to lose sight of Jesus in the midst of what He has done for us.

Sometimes, our abilities and accomplishments can be the thing that can hurt us the most, because it competes for our affection. We get so wrapped up in who we are that we lose sight of who He is. The issue was not, "Do you love Me more than the other disciples, or personal desires or lusts?" Instead, we must ask ourselves what it is that we really love. Where is our affection? Jesus was not talking to Peter (or us) about wicked things. He wasn't asking if Peter loved Him more than he loved his job. No, Jesus was asking Peter if he loved Jesus more than what He had just done for him. Are you more excited about what I can do than who I am?

The good ideas and deeds that flow from our lives often become too important. We become so busy with doing what's good that we miss what God is saying or doing in our lives. I've seen it happen to leaders when all was going well with their lives. I've even heard some say they deserve their success and fame. The moment we begin to start thinking that, we're in trouble. Once we begin to take for granted what God has invested in our lives, it won't be long before we begin to see what we could be like *without* Him.

How do we sidestep and avoid the temptation of competitor number two—our usefulness? Here are a few suggestions:

- **Who we are takes priority over what we do.** It is quite natural to define our self-worth by what we do for God instead of who we are in Christ Jesus. Our worth should be founded upon who we are as a result of God's love for us in Christ Jesus (see John 3:16; 1 John 4). Deceived by our natural abilities and human ingenuity, we often believe that we are indispensable to the work of God. We believe we are so useful to God that we are essential to His purposes. Quite the opposite is true. Our talents and gifts must be directed by godly character. We must submit to the process of being conformed and shaped into the image of Christ so that we function as a humble servant (see Phil. 2), instead of a high-profile performer. We must understand that humility and brokenness are the doorways into Father's kingdom.

- **Go for God ideas, not good ideas.** Remember that many of us have good ideas for serving God. But only the God ideas are profitable and essential to the fulfillment of God's purposes. Don't waste your time staying busy for God when you can redeem your time by being led by His Spirit (see Eph. 5:8-21).

- **Please God, not people.** When we get our eyes off God, we begin attempting to please others and ourselves. We become like the self-righteous religious leaders of Jesus' day, who "loved the praise of men more than the praise of God" (John 12:43, NKJV). What about you? Are you so impressed with your abilities that you serve to get the praises of others?

Competitor # 3: Our experiences in the Lord compete with our affection.

On the Mount of Transfiguration, after the glorious manifestation of Christ, Peter wanted to build three tabernacles as a memorial to that magnificent experience (see Matt. 17:1-8). Peter thought, "This is great! I like it here. Let's live here." Of course, Jesus said, "No. This is an experience for you to look back on, not a place for you to live." Experiences should propel us forward in the purposes of God rather than being a cause for camping out for long periods of time, as we contemplate the wonder of the experience.

Notice that as soon as the experience was over, Jesus took them down the mountain and immediately got back into the work.

Many of us desire to linger on in the profound experiences we've had in the Lord. However, that's not the purpose of those experiences. Many have pursued experience after experience, traveling around the world just to have an experience with God. Why do you think that is? I suppose that people are desperate and feel like they need these emotional lifts. But, I wonder, does God confine Himself to certain geographical locations? I don't think so. Spiritual experiences are great, but when we are tempted to stay too long in the afterglow of the experience, we will become distracted by it.

What then is the result of receiving the experience? Does it make one a stronger believer, a better leader, and give more wisdom? If it does, praise God. If not, then what is the point? As wonderful and confirming as spiritual experiences are, they are not self validating. They must bear fruit. Jesus doesn't tell us in John chapter 15 to have supernatural, spiritual experiences, as powerful as they may be. He does say that we are to bear fruit. I say it often, and I say it again. It's not about how many or how often people fall down; it is about what they do when they get back up.

Experiences are great, but there is always the danger that we will worship the experiences and not the Lord. "Let's build three tabernacles," Peter said. The place of the experience then becomes more important than the One we encountered. "No," Jesus replied, "let's go back down to where the people are, because that's where we need to go."

Jesus gives us the experiences to build us up as leaders so that when we get back down to the bottom of the mountain, it will qualify us and enhance what it is that He has called us to do. If your experiences aren't doing that, then you are worshiping the experience and not God.

How do we avoid the distraction of spiritual experiences? Let me suggest:

- **Seek God.** Praise God for the experience, but always seek God instead of the experience. King David sang, "When You said, 'Seek My face,' My heart said to You, 'Your face, Lord, I will seek'" (Ps. 27:8, NKJV).

- **Don't dwell in the experience.** The place of service for Jesus and the disciples wasn't in a dwelling place on top of the Mount of Transfiguration. God doesn't dwell in temples or tabernacles built by human hands (see Acts 17:24). Rather, God's Spirit dwells in us (see 1 Cor. 3:16) and gives us the power to serve and minister to others in His name.

DO YOU LOVE JESUS?

There are sins of commission (what you do), and there are sins of omission (what you don't do). At this point in life, I'm not sure which is worse, so I'll let you figure that out for yourself. As leaders, Jesus is saying that, if you love Him, don't get involved in counting the fish. He asks again, "Do you love Me or do you love what I do, what I give, or what I have? Why don't you love Me because of who I am?" Can you just love Him because of who He is? Why does it always have to be predicated by what He does, or what we want Him to do? Why not, as a leader, just love Him for who He is?

I love to preach. I love to serve. I like teaching, and I like driving the bus. I like doing what I do. But lookout!

"147, 148, 149."

"Hey, Peter!"

"150."

"Hey, hey!"

"153... hot dog!" Jesus just stands there, wondering why He even did the miracle.

"Why did I do this?" He asks.

It's not about the fish—the miracle. It's about the Miracle Worker. So, as a leader, don't count the fish.

LIFE PRINCIPLES IN THE CROSSHAIRS:

- **Focus on Jesus instead of on what He does for or through you.**

- **Don't waste your affections on seeking to get answers to your prayers.**

- **Don't fall in love with your usefulness, but rather, fall in love with the One who makes you useful.**

- **Don't seek spiritual experiences more than you seek Jesus.**

- **Be passionately in love with your first love—Jesus!**

As a leader, you must tell the people that you have feet of clay, but don't take off your shoes to show them. People must know that you are human and that you hurt, but people also look to you for strength and encouragement, especially those who follow you.

—Bill Wilson

Four rules of leadership...:

First, no matter how hard-fought the issue, never get personal. Don't say or do anything that may come back to haunt you on another issue, another day....

Second, do your homework. You can't lead without knowing what you're talking about....

Third, the American legislative process is one of give and take. Use your power as a leader to persuade, not intimidate....

Fourth, be considerate of the needs of your colleagues, even if they're at the bottom of the totem pole...."

—George H. Bush, Former President of the United States

Chapter 14

Don't Expose
Yourself to the People

*When the king heard the woman's words, he tore his robes. As
he went along the wall, the people looked, and there, underneath, he had sackcloth on his body* (2 Kings 6:30, NIV).

Jehoram became king of Judah upon the accidental death of
his brother, King Ahaziah. At times he was friendly with the Lord's
prophet Elisha, but at times he persecuted him. Sometimes he was
faithful to the Lord, but other times he blamed the Lord for problems caused by his own sins. He took steps against the cult of Baal
worship introduced by his father, King Ahab.

Time after time God displayed his power by rescuing Jehoram—
in a supply crisis at war, in preventing enemy raids on Israel's territory, in miraculously breaking a powerful siege, in many great
miracles worked by the prophet Elisha—and yet, in spite of all this
evidence, Jehoram never fully trusted the Lord.

Ben Hadad, king of Syria, had invaded Samaria and cut off
supplies to the whole nation. King Joram of Israel was devastated
because so many people had been killed during the fighting and
many others were dying from starvation. Scripture says that the
people had eaten all the animals and were even eating their young
to survive. When the king was confronted with these conditions,
he became so upset and grief-stricken that he tore off his clothes.

The Bible says that when he tore his clothes, the people of the
kingdom were shocked, but not because he tore off his clothes.
They were shocked because, in his mourning and despair, they
saw that he was wearing sackcloth under his royal garments. As he
tore off his royal garments, he exposed the condition of his heart to
the people.

Throughout biblical history, sackcloth was worn during times
of mourning. Sackcloth was visible because it was always worn on

the outside, so that others could see that you were in grief. The garments were usually made of goat hair, similar to a burlap bag, with holes cut out for the head and arms.

In Scripture, sackcloth and ashes were standards for all who mourned, except the king. The king never went into a public setting wearing anything but his royal garments. People expected the king to be above common problems, so it was a sign of weakness for him to behave otherwise. For the people to see a king in sackcloth and ashes would have created fear in the hearts of the people, or it would have given them cause to criticize the king.

However, when Joram saw this situation, he was so grief stricken that he tore at his clothes, and for the first time ever, the people saw that the king's heart was aching.

A LEADER'S DUTY

As a leader, the people must know that you have feet of clay. However, never take off your shoes to show them. They must know that you are human, and that you hurt and bleed just like they do, but they also look to you for strength and encouragement, especially those who follow you.

Many a leader has gotten hung because he was not discriminating enough in how he shared his problems with others. I am not advocating that a leader should never share with others the things that are happening in his life. What I am saying is that he must share with great discretion. A leader does need a couple people in his life with whom he can be open and honest.

On the other hand, he cannot be open and honest publicly. There are too many in the Body of Christ that are too immature to handle the personal life of their leader. The other problem is that there are unfortunately too many in the Body of Christ that will crucify the leaders once they are entrusted with that kind of personal information. Therefore, all of us should be very careful about the details of our personal lives.

Does this mean that a leader can never mourn or have days of discouragement? No! It simply means that you don't move out of your leadership role because of your own personal situation. You are still in leadership, so you must continue to lead. They must see you leading through your weaknesses. Your weaknesses will be obvious, but what must also be clear is that you know how to press through your weaknesses and remain steady and determined in your leadership.

Yes, you will have times of hurt and you will face battles; you will struggle and there will be problems. Nevertheless, when you face the people as their leader, let them know that, in spite of the battles and the pain, you will press forward. You can be hurt and in mourning, but remember that you are their leader. That's part of the job of leadership. The people need you and they need the strength that you bring to the situation.

YOUR SLIP IS SHOWING

When Israel was invaded, the king was so overcome with grief that he tore his clothes, revealing for the first time that the king's heart could hurt. The people didn't expect to see the king in sackcloth. They would rather have seen him in battle gear, ready to move out and bring the siege against them to an end. When the people saw the king's pain, it made their pain even worse.

When people see their leaders grieving, hope flees. They know from their own experience that grief consumes and over-powers even the simplest of tasks. They know that grief focuses attention on itself rather than other places. When the people of Israel saw their king grieving, they knew that he wasn't thinking about how to get out of the dreadful situation. They saw that the king was embroiled in their pain as well. It's true that kings grieve, as do pastors and leaders, but when leaders walk out front, they must leave their grief behind. As a leader, seek the help and grace of God in order to rise above the pressing problem.

I know that I cannot and would not want to share the details of my inner life with very many people. In fact, there are only a few that I trust with that information. Everyone must have some-one he can relate to as a leader. If a leader's child dies, or if he is betrayed by his best friend, or if his wife leaves him, how should he act in those situations?

It is important that people are able to see his grieving side, but they do not need to know all the details. They must see the grieving side as well as a confidence that is produced by grace.

Commoners could wear sackcloth on the outside for everyone to see, but not the king. Sure, leaders will have heartaches, but more is expected from them than from others. If you want your people to be positive, you must be positive. If you want your people to rise above the occasion, be faithful, and stick with it, then you must do so as well. This isn't done by crying and whining all over the place; that doesn't work. People are seeking a stable, secure leader—someone they can depend on. You would not be encouraged if you were on an airplane and the pilot came out and asked for directions. Nor would you be encouraged if your taxi driver took the wheel and said he was blind. You wouldn't be encouraged because you expect the leader to know what's going on and to have a plan.

LEADERS MUST LEAD

As a leader yourself, you set the pace. You chart the course and are expected to move out first. Being a leader means that you subordinate your needs to those of your followers. If the people don't have confidence in you, how do you expect them to follow? You can wear your sackcloth; just don't wear it on your sleeve!

The apostle Paul, in his letters to the churches, wrote of trials and struggles he was going through. However, the striking feature of Paul is not one of weakness, but is one of strength and triumph. Yes, he was beaten. Yes, he was thrown in prison. Yes, he was stoned and left for dead. Yes, he was shipwrecked and tossed in the open sea. But you never catch even a hint in his writings that he was giving up or that he didn't have a plan. However, he did speak often of his weaknesses. He used his weaknesses as an example to his followers. He told them often of his trials, scourgings, etc., and then he turned around and replied, "but I press on…". When he revealed his trials to the churches, he was not implying that he was giving up. I think he knew he was called, as a leader, to be an example to them. So by sharing his heartache, trials, sufferings, others following his lead would be strengthened, rather than disheartened, that "our leader is constantly pressed, persecuted, and struck down."

Proverbs 16:9 declares, "In his heart a man plans his course, but the Lord determines his steps" (NIV). You can be tossed and battle weary, but have a plan. You can be hurt and mournful, but have a plan. You can be facing the wall and unsure if you'll make it, but have a plan. See, with a plan, you've used the very thing that God has given you—your spirit that has a brain. Then, with your plan in mind, let Him direct your steps.

God has not given you a brain to just fill empty space in your skull; He's given you a brain to use. I'll tell you this, the more you use your brain, the sharper it becomes. Does this mean that you don't rely on the Holy Spirit to guide you? Of course not! The Spirit quickens your mind and helps you develop a plan that is consistent with God's Word. Then, as you execute the plan, you depend on the Spirit to direct your steps. A plan can have many ways of being fulfilled. Often, though, we only see one way. That is why it is so important to have God direct your steps. Let Him figure it out—just obey Him.

I WALKED A MILE WITH SORROW—BUT I KEPT GOING ON

I've had a lot of pain in my life. I've grieved and wondered if it was all worth it. I've been rejected over and over again by people I love and whom I thought loved me. I've been betrayed and sold out so that others could profit from what Metro Ministries has done. I, like Paul, have been beaten and left to die, shot, and shot at. Yet, even through all this, I've spoken of it only to motivate and encourage others, never to try to get people to feel sorry for me. I don't need anybody's pity.

Jesus is the author and finisher of *my* faith, not some two-faced man who is looking for a way to stiff me. Jesus is the only One who will not betray me or sell me out to others. Jesus binds my wounds and heals my broken heart; He comforts me when I mourn. It's easy to wear my sackcloth underneath my clothes because it's only important for the Lord to see it.

There are really only two kinds of people: those who wear sackcloth on the outside, and those who wear it underneath. I don't know what kind of leader you are. However, I do know that everyone will have heartache from time to time. How you handle it determines the stuff you are made of. Are you one to show everyone how bad you feel and help them feel just as bad? Or are you one who wears your mourning underneath while leading your people into the future God has for them? Remember, never let them see your underwear!

LIFE PRINCIPLES IN THE CROSSHAIRS:

- **Wear your sackcloth and morning on the inside.**
- **Lead others without showing them everything you feel on the inside.**
- **Let God direct your steps.**
- **Jesus will comfort you without exposing you to others.**

There is a great opportunity ahead of you. The world is bathed in fear, because they don't know what is going to happen to them. This is a window of opportunity and it's important to take advantage of the opportunities you have been given. There must be leaders that are willing to do whatever it takes to impact the world around them. We need men and women of character who are ready to take on this responsibility.

—Bill Wilson

Character cannot be developed in ease and quiet. Only through experience of trial and suffering can the soul be strengthened, ambition inspired, and success achieved.

—Helen Keller (1880–1968)

Watch your thoughts; they become words. Watch your words; they become actions. Watch your actions; they become habits. Watch your habits; they become character. Watch your character; it becomes your destiny.

—Unknown

CHAPTER 15

DO WHATEVER IT TAKES

Then the Spirit of the Lord came upon Jephthah. He crossed Gilead and Manasseh, passed through Mizpah of Gilead, and from there he advanced against the Ammonites. And Jephthah made a vow to the Lord: "If you give the Ammonites into my hands, whatever comes out of the door of my house to meet me when I return in triumph from the Ammonites will be the Lord's, and I will sacrifice it as a burnt offering."

Then Jephthah went over to fight the Ammonites, and the Lord gave them into his hands. He devastated twenty towns from Aroer to the vicinity of Minnith, as far as Abel Keramim. Thus Israel subdued Ammon.

When Jephthah returned to his home in Mizpah, who should come out to meet him but his daughter, dancing to the sound of tambourines! She was an only child. Except for her he had neither son nor daughter. When he saw her, he tore his clothes and cried, "Oh! My daughter! You have made me miserable and wretched, because I have made a vow to the Lord that I cannot break."

"My father," she replied, "you have given your word to the Lord. Do to me just as you promised, now that the Lord has avenged you of your enemies, the Ammonites. But grant me this one request," she said. "Give me two months to roam the hills and weep with my friends, because I will never marry."

"You may go," he said. And he let her go for two months. She and the girls went into the hills and wept because she would never marry. After the two months, she returned to her father and he did to her as he had vowed. And she was a virgin.(Judg. 11:29-39a, NIV).

Jephthah is one of my favorite Old Testament characters. Jephthah was to face the Ammonites in battle. He knew it would be a tough battle because the Ammonites were fierce warriors.

Jephthah knew that if he would have any chance at success, he would need God's help. Like every godly leader, Jephthah prayed for God's direction. He reached out to his Father, seeking His strength and support in order that he might be able to conquer his enemies.

Jephthah told God that if he would help Israel win the battle, then he would sacrifice the first thing that came out of his house to God as a burnt offering. To get the full impact of this story, it's important to understand how the houses were constructed in those days. The houses were rectangular and positioned in the center of a courtyard, surrounded by a wall several feet high. The courtyard around the outside of the house was where the owners kept their best animals; for example, the best ram, the best bullock, and the best he-goat. These were kept separate so they would not mix with the other animals.

You can understand what Jephthah was saying. Normally, the first thing that would come out of the house or courtyard was an animal. Therefore, Jephthah told God that if they won the battle he would offer the first animal (thing) that came out of the house (courtyard) as a sacrifice to Him.

As the story goes, Israel went to war and fought a fierce battle and in the end, Israel prevailed. As the army returned from this glorious victory, they eventually began to separate, as each man headed back to his own individual home. Jephthah, with a sound of victory still ringing in his ears, approached his house wondering what would be the first thing he would see. His heart was full of gratitude towards God for the success He gave them on the battlefield, and now he is prepared to keep his side of the bargain and fulfill his vow. As a true leader, he understood the significance and responsibility of fulfilling his vow to God. As he crests the hill, leading up to his home, he sees the house in the distance. His mind is racing now as he considers what animal will emerge from behind the courtyard wall. Will it be the best ram… the best bullock? What will it be?

As he draws near, to his utter devastation, the first thing that comes out of the house is not an animal at all; it is his only daughter. His weapons drop from his hands and Jephthah stands before her in stunned silence. Never, in his wildest dreams, did he think that this was how the story would end. Suddenly, his entire life and faith is on trial.

Theologians differ on the meaning of this Scripture and generally settle into one of two camps:

- Jephthah's daughter was kept as a virgin the rest of her life and never married.

- Jephthah actually sacrificed her.

You can choose to believe whichever one fits your level of commitment. I believe that he offered her as a burnt offering, just as the Scripture record says. I can find no other meaning of the Hebrew words, nor can I see any way out for Jephthah. To say the least, it was a time of reckoning for him and for her.

Without a doubt, there will come a time in the life of every man and woman when they will have to decide what they really believe, and what price they are willing to pay for it. In suspended animation, all time standing still, Jephthah is faced with making that decision. As he looks into the eyes of his daughter, and then looks into the heavens, his heart finds the strength to say yes to this, the ultimate test of his faith.

Jephthah made a difficult choice. We cannot always choose the easy road. Sometimes, it means we have to step out on the limb in faith, believing that God will support us as we reach out to Him from beyond our own natural abilities.

What Are You Like in Private?

Jephthah did not pray in public. This reality is critical to understanding this story and the principle behind it. Jephthah prayed in private. Nobody knew that he had prayed or that he had made that vow to God. However, he said that he opened his mouth unto the Lord and therefore couldn't go back. The commitments that we make in the private places must be fulfilled in the public places. Who you are in the concealed places will determine how you act in the crowded places. How you conduct yourself in the social places should be in harmony with how you behave in the secret places.

- How do you behave when you are alone?

- Is your public behavior consistent with your private behavior?

- Are you the same in the daylight as you are in the darkness?

Nobody would have known the difference, except Jephthah and God. Character is the key to this entire matter. You are what you really are when no one else is around. That is the true test of leadership. The true test of character is what happens in you when no one is there to witness it. Jephthah was willing to do whatever it took to keep his vow to the Lord—I wish we had a few people like that left. Wouldn't it be nice if we had people that would say, "God, I've made a decision, this is what I'm going to do. No matter what happens, no matter what it costs, no matter what it takes, I'm going to keep my commitment to You."

It would be quite significant to the cause of Christ if we had people that love Him enough to say, "Lord, here am I, send me." When the coals were taken off the altar and touched Isaiah's lips, something happened. Isaiah responded by saying, "Here am I, Lord, send me." Send me! What a bold statement to make to the Lord. In other words, "God, use me. No matter what the price or the sacrifice, I am willing for you to do in me and with me whatever you want."

God is looking for miracle workers today—is that you? I wonder if Paul's parents knew that he would write the majority of the New Testament when he was born. Who knows your full potential, but God? Something can happen with you just like it did with Isaiah and with Paul. But it will require the resolve of a Jephthah and the courage of a Paul to walk out that commitment.

YOU HAVE NOTHING TO FEAR!

There is a great opportunity ahead of you. The world is bathed in fear, because they don't know what is going to happen to them. This is a window of opportunity and it's important to take advantage of the opportunities you have been given. There must be leaders that are willing to do whatever it takes to impact the world around them. We need men and women of character who are ready to take on this responsibility.

What keeps you from taking the next step with God? What keeps you in the boat instead of stepping over the side and walking toward Jesus, like Peter did? Jesus is saying, "Come!" Will you hear and obey, or will fear paralyze you with inaction?

You have nothing to fear. Don't be afraid of your past; Jesus has forgiven you. What's behind you does not determine what is before you. Don't fear the present; no weapon formed against you will prosper. The present moment is the doorway into your destiny. Don't fear the future; Jesus is the Alpha and Omega. He's already been where you are going. Your future is already in God's past. He has already been there and you can trust in Him. Paul writes, "For God has not given us a spirit of fear, but of power and of love and of a sound mind" (2 Tim. 1:7). Let go of fear, grab hold of your destiny, and step into God's future for you.

What that means for you, I have no idea. Only you know where God is taking you. Only you know what it might demand. So, before you read further, just put the book down and talk to the Lord.

Pray this prayer out loud as you seek God's guidance and counsel:

> "Father, I love You and I thank You. I pray that, as I think on these things I must confront in my life, You will strengthen and encourage me. Lord, the world is watching. I've heard it said that the world has yet to see what a man or woman totally committed to God can do. I would like to be that person. I would like to be that person, totally committed to You, for no other reason than because I love You. Lord, I pray that You'll help me. In Jesus' name, Amen."

LIFE PRINCIPLES IN THE CROSSHAIRS:

- **How you conduct yourself in the social places should be in harmony with how you behave in the secret place.**

- **No matter what the price or the sacrifices, begin to trust your Father enough to be willing to say yes.**

- **You have nothing to fear. Don't be afraid of your past; Jesus has forgiven you. What's behind you does not determine what is before you.**

- **Don't fear the present; no weapon formed against you will prosper. The present moment is your doorway into your destiny.**

- **Don't fear the future; Jesus is the Alpha and Omega. He's already been where you are going. Your future is already in God's past, and He waits for you.**

PART 4

PRINCIPLES OF GOD'S PREVAILING PRESENCE

All through the Scriptures, the great men and women of God have been consistent and focused in their pursuit of the presence of God. They have learned through personal experience the power of God's prevailing presence in their lives. The presence of God in their lives has determined whether there would be great victories or horrible defeats.

Where does one turn when he has failed? Cain fled from the presence of God while David pursued the presence of God. David sought that place where the enemy could not go after him. Jesus said on one occasion that, where two or three are gathered, there He is in the midst of them. God promises His presence in the midst of our friendships. The friendship of Jonathan and David illustrates the favor of God upon true friendship. Sometimes our friends will have to speak a challenging word into our lives. David and Nathan teach us to trust the word that comes from a true friend. Often, God is present in that word. Finally, in the last two chapters, we will look at the classic story on the presence of God— bringing back the Ark to Jerusalem. David and Obed-Edom will teach us much about the commitment and the blessing of living in the presence of God.

There are places where your enemy cannot follow you. Therefore, instead of standing around trying to fight the enemy in your own strength and on his turf with your weapons, go to a place where the enemy cannot go. That place is simply—God's presence.

—Bill Wilson

O my God, since Thou art with me, and I must now, in obedience to Thy commands, apply my mind to these outward things, I beseech Thee to grant me the grace to continue in Thy Presence; and to this end do Thou prosper me with Thy assistance, receive all my works, and possess all my affections.

—Brother Lawrence

If God is present at every point in space, if we cannot go where He is not, cannot even conceive of a place where He is not, why then has not that Presence become the one universally celebrated fact of the world?

—A.W. Tozer

CHAPTER 16

STAY AROUND GOD'S PLACE

Thou wilt show me the path of life: in Thy presence is fulness of joy; at Thy right hand there are pleasures for evermore (Ps. 16:11, KJV).

Why are you in despair, O my soul? And why have you become disturbed within me? Hope in God, for I shall again praise Him for the help of His presence (Ps. 42:5, NASB).

Let us come before His presence with thanksgiving, let us shout joyfully to Him with psalms (Ps. 95:2, NASB).

When my mother died, I went back to St. Petersburg, Florida, to take care of the funeral arrangements. While I was there, I received a phone call from a woman in her eighties, a lady I knew from many years before. She had been a missionary in Africa, and she was living in one of the missionary homes in the area. When I was a boy, I remember that I had stayed there quite often when I had nowhere to live and was floating back and forth between homes.

My friend was very old now. She had been on the mission field most of her life, a life that was very hard. Some Christians had been very unkind to her, so she rarely received visitors. It was too painful. So, I was surprised to hear that she wanted to see me. It had been nearly twenty years since I had seen her last. I was a little shocked when I saw the condition of her health. When I walked in, she was sitting in an old rocker and her eyes were closed. I learned later that she had a disease that caused deterioration of the muscles above her eyelids so she could no longer hold them open. This woman had heard about my mother's death. She said that she had called me there to tell me something very important. I quickly realized that this would probably be the last time we spoke together. Therefore, her words took on even greater importance.

NEVER LEAVE THE PRESENCE OF GOD

She told me that she knew what I was doing because she had followed my life. She told me that she remembered what had happened to me when I was young, and she knew how hard it had been. At this point in the conversation, she told me to come close. She wanted to see my face when she spoke next. In order for us to look each other in the eyes, I had to use my fingers to hold open her eyes. Time was standing still in the quietness of that little room. I could hear my own heart beating, and could smell the scent of old age permeating the air. Looking into my eyes, she said that, if I was going to make it in the ministry, *I must never leave the presence of God.*

I can't tell you how significant that day was in my life. I've had a lot of very significant things happen in my life, but this was obviously something that would leave an imprint on my soul for the rest of my life. I didn't really know what to say in response to her challenge. I was getting uncomfortable because of the seriousness of the moment. So, we talked a little while longer, and then I left.

This was a *kairos* moment for me—one of those moments in time that can never be recreated or duplicated. A *kairos* moment is a special moment in the midst of many moments. It is a critical time, in which eternity intersects earthly time. If you miss that moment in time, it's missed for eternity. I've had many of these over the years, and am smart enough to know that, when the opportunity is there, you'd better latch onto it. *"If you're going to make it, don't ever leave the presence of God"*—I had experienced a *kairos* moment in the presence of an old friend.

WHAT IS THE PRESENCE OF GOD?

The phrase, "presence of God," conjures up things in my mind—things that I was taught when very young, things that may or may not have been accurate. "The presence of God" has always been somewhat of an enigma for me because I've never really quite understood it. Is the presence of God something that you go to, or does it comes to you?

I've heard it preached both ways, and I am still confused.

That moment launched a quest of a lifetime for me. Most of the principles taught in this book and most of the sermons I preach come from the experiences that I've had in the pursuit and experience of His presence. That has, in many different ways, directed my life. Something will happen, or somebody will say something that pushes me into a search to figure it out for myself. So, what's the difference between those who make it and those who don't make it on the spiritual journey?

> So Cain went out from the Lord's presence and lived in the land of Nod, east of Eden (Gen. 4:16, NIV).

> Do not cast me from Your presence or take Your Holy Spirit from me (Ps. 51:11, NIV).

Two men—Cain and David—had both committed murder and were standing on the precipice of a great tragedy. Both men had committed the unthinkable and were dangerously close to experiencing total ruin in their lives. Cain had allowed his rejection and anger to lead him to the murder of his brother. David had allowed lust and passion to lead him to the execution of one of his own soldiers.

Although in similar situations, one man runs away from the presence of God, while the other one begs not to lose it. Interesting, isn't it? Cain makes the decision to leave the presence of God and we don't hear from him anymore. David makes the decision not to leave God's presence and faces the horrible implications of his sin. In his pursuit of the presence of God, he finds Father's forgiveness and is restored. What makes the difference between those who succeed and those who fail in the spiritual journey? I believe it is the presence of God.

I've heard it said: "If you don't feel close to God, guess who moved?" This is a tremendous truth. Often people say they don't feel close to God. I've got news for you. It's not God's fault—it's yours. His presence is always there, but we are not always before Him. It is said of Brother Lawrence, "... by this short and sure method, he exercised himself in the knowledge and love of God, resolving to use his utmost endeavor to live in a continual sense of His Presence, and, if possible, never to forget Him more."

A CAT CAN'T FLY

David begged to stay in God's presence, and yet he wasn't "right with God" (as we say it) when he was begging for the return of the presence of God in his life! We wrongly think that being in the presence of God means being right with God. Being right with God has nothing to do with being in God's presence. The question you must answer is simple: *Do you want to be in His presence?*

To be in His presence, you must be around God's place. In other words, go where God is. I used to preach a sermon entitled, "A Cat Can't Fly." Birds usually have enough sense not to square off with a cat. If a cat tries to get to a bird, the bird simply flies to a place where the cat cannot go. There are places where your enemy cannot follow you. Therefore, instead of standing around, trying to fight the enemy in your own strength and on his turf with your weapons, go to a place where the enemy cannot go. That place is simply God's presence. Do you want to be in God's presence? Be around God's place.

Cain left the presence of God and David never did. Don't do what many Christians do when they fail. They often stay away from church, worship services, and fellowship with God's people. They often withdraw from prayer and the Word. They choose to sulk in their own sorrow rather than pursue the presence of the very One who can heal and restore them. Retreating from God's presence is the last thing that you want to do when you have failed.

When you're in the midst of a battle, stay close to the ones who can encourage and support you. Stay in the environment of God's presence, where His Holy Spirit can minister to you. David and Cain both committed murder. One stayed in God's presence, while the other one left it. Who do you think found the forgiveness he needed? Was it the one who fled, or the one who stayed?

A PLACE OF LOVE IN THE PRESENCE OF GOD

A couple of years ago, some monthly supporters from Texas came to visit the ministry. While they were here, we were fitting one of our kids, who was pregnant, with a maternity dress, and were getting her ready to be sent to a home for unwed mothers. One of the visiting women heard about what we were doing. She came to me and said that, when she got back to her church, she would recommend that they stop sending us monthly support, and that she wanted me to know about it before she left.

When I asked why she would do that, she said it was because we bought the maternity dress for that girl; she felt like we were condoning her sin. I told her we do not condone her sin, but were trying to save the lives of both the baby and the young girl. I told her that, when someone makes a mistake, unlike other churches, we don't just throw them out.

When someone is in a mess, the church needs to circle the wagons around them, pray over them, love them, and help them.

The problem is that it's much easier to sit in the seat of the scornful (see Ps. 1:1), looking down on the guilty, and pointing religious fingers at them. It is very difficult both to live in the presence of God and be judgmental.

If ever there is a time when the Church needs to love people, it's during the times of their failure, when they feel so rejected. If they don't get it from the Church, where in God's name are they going to get it? Where can they find love outside the Church? The world? The world uses people—chews them up and spits them out! Yet in so many cases, the Church isn't much different. The Church was always meant to be the place of the Presence, where those who are hurting and those who have failed will be able to encounter God's love as it is manifested through His people.

A church without love has nothing. God is love and where He is present, that love will be manifested. If that love is not there, maybe it is a sign that He isn't there either. We cannot continue to reject people just because they aren't like us. What would have happened if the church had done that with you? Where would you be? It's now or never. Do we want God's presence or not? If you want to be in God's presence, be around His place, as painful as it can be at times, and as goofy as His Church is sometimes. His place is His people, gathered in His name. When they gather, Jesus promises to be there.

For where two or three are gathered together in My name, I am there in the midst of them (Matt. 18:20, NKJV).

LIFE PRINCIPLES IN THE CROSSHAIRS:

- **When you have failed, begin the journey back to God, not away from Him.**

- **To be effective in ministry, you must never leave the presence of God.**

- **The difference between those who succeed and fail in the Christian walk is a matter of remaining in the presence of God.**

- **The church was always meant to be a place of His presence, where those who are hurting and those who have failed will be able to encounter God's love as it is manifested through His people.**

When a Christian sins and falls away from God, his life begins to unravel and deteriorate. What he must understand is that guilt and shame do not come from God; they are tools of satan. The Holy Spirit convicts people of their sins; He does not condemn or shame them.

—Bill Wilson

A pervasive sense of shame is the ongoing premise that one is fundamentally bad, inadequate, defective, unworthy, or not fully valid as a human being.

—Lewis Smedes

The glory of friendship is not the outstretched hand, nor the kindly smile...it's the spiritual inspiration that comes to one when he discovers that someone else believes in him and is willing to trust him with his friendship.

—Ralph Waldo Emerson

CHAPTER 17

STAY AROUND GOD'S PEOPLE

Create in me a pure heart, O God, and renew a steadfast spirit within me. Do not cast me from Your presence or take Your Holy Spirit from me. Restore to me the joy of Your salvation and grant me a willing spirit, to sustain me. Then I will teach transgressors Your ways, and sinners will turn back to You (Ps. 51:10-13, NIV).

Jonathan made David vow again because of his love for him, because he loved him as he loved his own life (1 Sam. 20:17, NASB).

As soon as Cain sinned, he changed associates and moved somewhere else (see Gen. 4:15-16). It's not unusual that when people make a mistake, the first thing they do is to look for a way to change groups. They find new friends or, at least, forsake their former friends. Often, they will leave church under the guise of being "too busy" to attend. Sometimes, they just drop out of sight and become solitary figures, with little or no human contact. When we have failed or sinned, it is the nature within us that drives us to separate ourselves from others. We are sure that the presence of other people in our lives will only accentuate the pain that we are already feeling. The shame that grips our hearts drives us from the very pastures that were meant for our healing.

David stayed in God's presence. Psalm 51 is a classic dialogue concerning David's passion toward God. David knew that he had sinned and that his actions had caused pain for many people. He knew that he had grieved God as well. But he also understood that there would be no relief for him by running away. In many ways, he was so accustomed to the presence of God that he could not imagine another day in his life without the sweet presence of Father.

David still went to the temple to worship. He still surrounded himself with singers that continually sang praises to God from the Psalms. David continued to seek the presence of the Lord. This principle is very important to grasp because everyone, at one time or another, is going to be faced with a decision of whether to stay or flee.

HANDLING GUILT AND SHAME

When a Christian sins and falls away from God, his life begins to unravel and deteriorate. The first feelings that surge into his soul are guilt and shame. Drowning in the intensity of that guilt and shame, he finds it difficult to be around other Christians, especially those with whom he used to associate. Bearing his guilt and shame, he begins to be less and less visible, often leaving the fellowship of other Christians completely. Now there are two reasons why this happens. First, Christians have not been well known for their gracious reception of the broken sinner. We are more known for our judgment than our loving care. Secondly, the wounded are often so humiliated by their failure that being in the presence of others only adds to their shame. In their defeat they run, and may not return.

Guilt and shame do not come from God; they are tools of Satan. The Holy Spirit convicts people of their sin; He does not condemn or shame them. Only one stands condemned, satan. Regarding conviction, Jesus said:

> But I tell you the truth: It is for your good that I am going away. Unless I go away, the Counselor will not come to you; but if I go, I will send Him to you. When He comes, He will convict the world of guilt in regard to sin and righteousness and judgment: in regard to sin, because men do not believe in Me; in regard to righteousness, because I am going to the Father, where you can see Me no longer; and in regard to judgment, because the prince of this world now stands condemned (John 16:7-11, NIV).

Regarding shame, David said:

> To You, O Lord, I lift up my soul; in You I trust, O my God. Do not let me be put to shame, nor let my enemies triumph over me. No one whose hope is in You will ever be put to shame, but they will be put to shame who are treacherous without excuse (Ps. 25:1-3, NIV).

When you understand that it is satan (and not God) who heaps the guilt and shame on you, then you can deal with guilt and shame through confession and repentance, and get on with your life. You will not find the permanent healing you need on a counselor's couch; you will only find it in the lap of the Father. It's unfortunate that people are so blind in their walks with God that they believe He is the author of condemnation. It is clear that the Church has not marketed this message very well. In fact, with their own judgment and condemnation, they have produced a lot of misinformation about God.

Nevertheless, there are people who do genuinely care, and it will be these people that you must find. Surround yourself with believers who love God, not the kind that become the mouthpiece of the enemy by shouting words of shame and condemnation at you. True friends are a part of Father's key to bring you back to healing and restoration.

Shame and guilt can be dealt with directly and simply. Don't get caught up in ritual or become super-religious about shame and guilt. Nobody ever got right at the altar. You make a decision to get right at the altar—that begins the process. First of all, *confess.* Confess is agreeing with God that you are wrong and He is right. His way is the only way and your way falls short every time. Scripture promises, "If we confess our sins, He is faithful and just to forgive us our sins and to cleanse us from all unrighteousness" (1 John 1:9, NKJV).

However, complete restoration doesn't stop with confession. Confession cleans you up, but you also have to change. That's where repentance comes into the picture. I often see people come to an altar and confess their sins, and then leave the service and keep on living the old way, with the old sinful habits. They haven't changed. They were stirred, but did not change. Repentance means change. When you repent, you change directions; you turn completely away from the sin you have confessed. So, not only do you need to be cleaned up from your sin through confession; you must also repent—stop that sin and begin doing what's right. Too many people want relief from guilt and shame, but they resist genuine change because repentance and change require them to live and act differently.

Remember that the power to make a change does not emerge out of your flesh. It is a product of your submission to the spiritual power that is resident in you as a gift of God. Are you sincere?

Do you really want to rid yourself of shame and guilt? Then confess and repent. Admit what's wrong. Quit doing it and start doing what's right!

CHOOSE YOUR FRIENDS CAREFULLY

Having idiots—Proverbs calls them "fools"—for friends is the fastest way to get yourself into a spiritual, relational, or financial bind. I don't go out for coffee and I don't chitchat after the Sunday meeting. This after-church "fellowship" usually becomes a hotbed of gossip. People get together and decide what to have for lunch, and it usually includes some people they all know. This thinly disguised fellowship is nothing more than a time to spread their evil gossip. Their conversation sounds like, "We need to pray for the 'you-know-whos,' because of the terrible time they're having after his affair with the secretary...Oh! You didn't know about the affair? Well, it's over now, but they still need prayer."

About four years ago, I was debating whether I could even continue to speak in public. I was so angry at the way "church people" hurt one another. I struggled with loving people who willfully hurt others by professing God's love at church but don't back their profession up with "living it" during the week. "How can they say what they say, yet live how they live? I don't understand." This is nothing new, but I guess I was just tired of the foolishness.

I've got to continually guard my attitude because, if I'm not careful, I say things that need not be said. I have seen things that most people, especially preachers, have never seen, and I know people will not understand—by and large. They don't really care. That angers me. Therefore, I have questioned whether I could continue doing ministry, but then concluded, once again, that I must. I need to be around godly people. I need the interaction I get from people who are passionate about God and genuinely care about me. I can be gruff and abrasive and sometimes that is offensive to people, but I still need the love and concern of my brothers and sisters in the Lord that do get it.

Remember the advice of Psalm 1? Here it is again:

Oh, the joys of those who do not follow the advice of the wicked, or stand around with sinners, or join in with scoffers. But they delight in doing everything the Lord wants; day and night they think about his law. They are like trees planted along the riverbank, bearing fruit each season without fail. Their leaves never wither, and in all they do, they prosper (Ps. 1:1-3, NLT).

I really don't have a lot of interaction with nice people. My life isn't lived like that; in fact, my life is very close to that of a cop. The only time someone calls a cop is when they're in trouble. People usually don't call the cops to tell them they are doing a good job, or to invite them over for dinner. People call the cops when there is trouble. This is how I live and, after seeing 22 murders, and having viewed the good, the bad, and the ugly of church life, it's easy to become hard and cynical. So, I must constantly guard against it. I need to have friends in my life that will help me not go too far down the road of cynicism.

By nature, I'm an emotional person, but I've had to make myself hard to survive on the street. I've searched for the middle ground, because I don't want to become an emotional basket case who is no good to anyone. Nor do I want to become so hardened and cynical that that I'm no good to anyone that way either. I've had to find this middle ground where people don't run over me while I remain tender to the things of God.

As hard as it is to be around certain kinds of Christians, you still need to have people that you can joke with and who are genuinely nice to you. It's tempting to think that it would be easier to just back out of it and become a recluse, but you can't do that. I've seen many old preachers go down that road. It's easy to do. If you do, you're in trouble. You need to be around God's people. You need to be in His presence through other people.

According to First Corinthians 12, we are all part of Christ's body ,and each one has a specific role to play. Just because you're different from me doesn't mean you aren't necessary, and vice versa. Everyone is important in the Body of Christ, the Church. Every different perspective is necessary in order to see the whole.

WE NEED ONE ANOTHER

Remember the story about the blind men and the elephant? Five blind men were told to touch an elephant and describe it. One touched the tail and said this creature was like a rope. Another touched a leg and said the creature was like a tree. Still another touched its side and determined the creature was like a wall. One touched the trunk and said the creature was a hollow tube, while one touched an ear and said the elephant was like a big fan.

Were any of them wrong in what they touched and described? No. Did any of them have a complete picture? No. This is the church! We must all live and grow together so that we "see" what God is doing and can cooperate with Him in it.

Do you want to be in God's presence? One of the ways is to surround yourself with people who are passionate about God and His purposes. Get close to somebody who's close to God. Remember, the Church is like Noah's ark. It was stinking and smelly, and had a bunch of weird animals in it. The Church is like the ark—stinking and smelling. But it's still the best boat afloat. It's filled with imperfect people, but we serve a perfect God. Do you want to be in God's presence? Get around His people; get close to someone who is close to Him.

LIFE PRINCIPLES IN THE CROSSHAIRS:

- **Shame and guilt come from satan, not God.**

- **Deal with shame and guilt through confession and repentance.**

- **True friends are a part of Father's key to bring you back to healing and restoration.**

- **Surround yourself with people who are passionate about God and His purposes.**

- **Stay around positive Christians who really love God and others.**

All of us need a person who will pray for us and speak God's word to us when we have blind spots of sin in our lives. Don't isolate yourself from good and faithful friends who will confront you and help you overcome the obstacles in your life. Seek them out. Stay around them and allow their influence to change you.

—Bill Wilson

It is the Law of Influence that we become like those whom we habitually admire: these had become like because they habitually admired. Through all the range of literature, of history, and biography this law presides. Men are all mosaics of other men.

—Henry Drummond

It is one of the severest tests of friendship to tell your friend his faults. So to love a man that you cannot bear to see a stain upon him, and to speak painful truth through loving words, that is friendship.

—Henry Ward Beecher

Chapter 18

Stay Around God's Priests

*The Lord sent Nathan to David. When he came to him, he said,
"There were two men in a certain town, one rich and the other
poor. The rich man had a very large number of sheep and cattle, but the poor man had nothing except one little ewe lamb he
had bought. He raised it, and it grew up with him and his children. It shared his food, drank from his cup and even slept in
his arms. It was like a daughter to him.*

*"Now a traveler came to the rich man, but the rich man re-
frained from taking one of his own sheep or cattle to prepare a
meal for the traveler who had come to him. Instead, he took the
ewe lamb that belonged to the poor man and prepared it for the
one who had come to him."*

*David burned with anger against the man and said to Nathan,
"As surely as the Lord lives, the man who did this deserves to
die! He must pay for that lamb four times over, because he did
such a thing and had no pity."*

*Then Nathan said to David, "You are the man! This is what
the Lord, the God of Israel, says: 'I anointed you king over Israel, and I delivered you from the hand of Saul. I gave your
master's house to you, and your master's wives into your
arms. I gave you the house of Israel and Judah. And if all this
had been too little, I would have given you even more. Why did
you despise the word of the Lord by doing what is evil in his
eyes? You struck down Uriah the Hittite with the sword and
took his wife to be your own. You killed him with the sword of
the Ammonites'"* (2 Sam. 12:1-9, NIV).

As most of us do, after David had committed this grotesque
sin, he went into an immediate cover-up. Those that knew about
his sin might have been too afraid to confront him. But there was
one person in his life that was not afraid to challenge his old
friend, the king. Nathan was bold in his approach to the king, and

his words convicted David of his sin. Imagine the atmosphere in the king's court that day. Nathan spoke truth to the king, and the truth hurt. The king holds the power of life and death in his hands. He could have ordered the execution of Nathan, but something inside him would not let him leave the man of God. Therefore, when Nathan spoke, David had enough sense to listen. It was at that point, when confronted by the man of God, that David's life began to turn around. Never underestimate the power of God's word as it comes through a godly friend. It just might be the very word that will save your life.

Nobody likes to be confronted, but everyone has been. If you haven't, you probably should have been confronted at some time in your life. Nobody likes to be told they are wrong or have their sins pointed out; it hurts and is embarrassing. It becomes your choice to either get close to the man of God and listen, or to walk away and suffer the consequences. If you can't discipline yourself, someone else will be forced to do it for you. If your godly friends don't choose to confront your sin, then they confirm or agree with your sin. It is the good friends who will speak God's words into your life.

Christ has placed in His church apostles, prophets, evangelists, pastors, and teachers (see Eph. 4:11). He did this for a purpose:

> *To prepare God's people for works of service, so that the body of Christ may be built up until we all reach unity in the faith and in the knowledge of the Son of God and become mature, attaining to the whole measure of the fullness of Christ. Then we will no longer be infants, tossed back and forth by the waves, and blown here and there by every wind of teaching and by the cunning and craftiness of men in their deceitful scheming. Instead, speaking the truth in love, we will in all things grow up into Him who is the Head, that is, Christ* (Eph. 4:12-15, NIV).

These ministers, men and women of God, fulfill vital roles in the church. Ignoring their counsel or correction brings with it the trouble associated with disobedience. David sinned, first with Bathsheba, then with her husband, Uriah. Time had passed before Nathan ever came to him, because God was convicting him first.

RECEIVE CONVICTION AND CORRECTION

When one sins, a spiritual process begins almost immediately. The Holy Spirit begins to convict the heart of the person, trying to lead him or her to repentance. If the person turns a deaf "ear" to the Spirit, or their heart becomes hardened, then God will find other means, including people, to get their attention. If they refuse to listen to another person, then they are turned over to the devil, according to First Corinthians 5:5, so that the sinful nature can be destroyed and their soul saved.

David ignored the voice of the Spirit, so he was not in harmony with the spiritual process at work within him. Because of his disobedience, he paid a price. His refusal to listen to God took him out of the covering of blessing that had been over him since his youth. The discord of sin and separation from God will cause all sorts of ailments and issues that must be dealt with.

Psalm 32:1-5 describes David's condition when he finally admitted his sin to Nathan:

Blessed is he whose transgressions are forgiven, whose sins are covered. Blessed is the man whose sin the Lord does not count against him and in whose spirit is no deceit. When I kept silent, my bones wasted away through my groaning all day long. For day and night Your hand was heavy upon me; my strength was sapped as in the heat of summer. Then I acknowledged my sin to You and did not cover up my iniquity. I said, "I will confess my transgressions to the Lord"—and You forgave the guilt of my sin (NIV).

Staying close to the godly people helps prevent the ignoring of sin and transgression. Paul said in 1 Corinthians 11:1, "Imitate me, just as I also imitate Christ" (NKJV). The men and women of God set the example to follow. They have their eyes on Christ and walk according to what they see. As they imitate Christ, they will speak into your life and expose areas of darkness and sin that must be exposed and dealt with.

CONFRONTATION HELPS YOU SEE "BLIND SPOTS"

When Nathan confronted David, the atmosphere changed in the palace. David's own words best describe it:

Have mercy on me, O God, according to Your unfailing love; according to Your great compassion blot out my transgressions.

Wash away all my iniquity and cleanse me from my sin. For I know my transgressions, and my sin is always before me. Against You, You only, have I sinned and done what is evil in Your sight, so that You are proved right when You speak and justified when You judge. Surely I was sinful at birth, sinful from the time my mother conceived me. Surely You desire truth in the inner parts; You teach me wisdom in the inmost place. Cleanse me with hyssop, and I will be clean; wash me, and I will be whiter than snow. Let me hear joy and gladness; let the bones You have crushed rejoice. Hide Your face from my sins and blot out all my iniquity. Create in me a pure heart, O God, and renew a steadfast spirit within me. Do not cast me from Your presence or take Your Holy Spirit from me. Restore to me the joy of Your salvation and grant me a willing spirit, to sustain me (Ps. 51:1-12, NIV).

FRIENDS CAN SEE OUR BLIND SPOTS WHEN WE CAN'T

David had a blind spot in his spiritual vision. We cannot see our sins or failures the way others can see them. We need others to help us diagnose our sicknesses—both physical and spiritual. Physicians tell us that they do a very poor job at self-diagnosis. When they get sick, they go to another doctor.

Years ago, a Christian author wrote that sin was the deadliest addiction. Why is that? Simply because sin comes with a built-in "denial reflex." The whole thing started in the beginning of time in that ancient garden. After Adam and Eve's sin, the whole process of hiding and blaming began. Rather than confront our sin, we chose to either hide it from others or blame others. Both attitudes will lead you down a slippery slope of self-destruction. Like all addictions, once we start down that dangerous pathway, our desires only increase as we seek greater and greater carnal pleasure. It's amazing that when we are sinning, we deny that we have a problem. It's a blind spot in our spiritual lives that others can see clearly. David lived in denial until Nathan exposed his "blind spot." Sin denies, rationalizes, and excuses our behavior.

What we need are friends who will speak the truth to us in love. In Proverbs we read, "Wounds from a friend are better than many kisses from an enemy" (Prov. 27:6, NLT). Those wounds are like a surgeon's scalpel that seeks to remove diseased tissue, so that the body can heal. While the surgery may be temporarily painful, the long-term results are healing and wholeness. The same is true spiritually. Friends who speak the truth in love to us, confronting us with our blind spots, may cause some pain initially. But, the truth is, the long-term results of their confrontation bring relational and spiritual healing into our lives.

That's what happened with David and Nathan. Nathan's godly rebuke, spoken in love for both David and God, brought needed repentance and change in David's relationship both with God and with others. David developed a contrite, new, and right spirit. So welcome loving rebuke, correction, and confrontation from friends. When they expose your blind spots to you, they are helping you see what needs to change so that you can grow and mature in Christ.

Are You Willing to Listen and to Change?

David found healing for his body, his soul, and spirit when he confessed his sin and turned from it. He could not undo what he had done, no more than you or I can. However, he was able to find power in his repentance. Nathan was bold and spoke the word of the Lord to David. David responded because he was willing to listen to the man that God had sent. Through his response, he could be lifted out of the "hiding and blaming" game and get back on the track with his destiny. What about you? Are you willing to hear the voice of God through another?

It's one thing to be ignorant of your sin, but it's another to try and hide it. Every time you back away from God and His word, you stand in danger of judgment. Listen to the voice of God, spoken through the Nathan who comes your way. Heed His call to repentance and return to the favor of the Lord. God has set in your life people who are concerned for your eternal safety. They speak in obedience to God, and bring words of life to those who are perishing.

David never left the man of God. If he would have, he never would have heard him. David knew the secret; he stayed by the man of God and listened to him. All of us need a person who will pray for us and speak God's word to us when we have blind spots of sin in our lives. Don't isolate yourself from good and faithful friends who will confront you and help you overcome the obstacles in your life. Seek them out. Stay around them, and allow their influence to change you.

LIFE PRINCIPLES IN THE CROSSHAIRS:

- Be willing to receive confrontation and correction from friends who love God and you.

- Don't deny your blind spots and sin. Avoid the hiding and blaming game.

- Stay close to the spiritual friends in your life who hear from God and speak the truth in love to you.

- When confronted with the truth, be willing to repent and change.

The natural inclination of man is to go where he thinks it best to and to do what he thinks is best, even if it isn't. However, in God's presence, all that changes. The will of man is conquered by the will of God.

—Bill Wilson

But thinking is not enough. Men are made to worship also, to bow down and adore in the presence of the mystery inexpressible. Man's mind is not the top pea, of his nature. Higher than his mind is his spirit, that something within him which can engage the supernatural, which under the breath of the Spirit can come alive and enter into conscious communion with heaven, can receive the divine nature and hear and feel and see the ineffable wonder that is God....

—A. W. Tozer

God often takes a course for accomplishing His purposes directly contrary to what our narrow views would prescribe. He brings a death upon our feelings, wishes, and prospects when He is about to give us the desire of our hearts.

—John Newton

CHAPTER 19

IF YOU LIVE IN HIS PRESENCE, YOU WILL FIND HIS PURPOSE

Some of the fiercest enemies of the children of Israel were the Philistines. They were a continual thorn in the side of Israel for many years, and the two nations had fought many battles against each other. Right before the prophet Samuel came on the scene, a great battle took place involving these two. In the first skirmish, Israel was soundly beaten, with 4000 men dying on the battlefield. Fearing that they would be totally crushed by the Philistines, the elders of Israel came up with a desperate plan. They decided to transport the ark of the covenant from its resting place in Shiloh and bring it onto the battlefield. They thought that, by having the ark with them, the presence of God would come into their midst, and God would fight for them.

The ark of the covenant was a box about two feet wide and four feet long. The top had two seraphs, the sides had rings through which poles were placed to carry it, and it was covered entirely with gold. Inside were the Ten Commandments, a golden pot of manna, and Aaron's rod that had budded. The ark was the most precious piece of furniture in the Tabernacle. It literally represented the presence of God, and was carried with Israel wherever they went. The ark's resting place was in the Holy of Holies in the Tabernacle; it was later placed in the Temple, in Solomon's time.

There was just one little problem with this hastily devised plan—they didn't ask God what He thought about it. Evidently, God was not impressed with their plan and was not present at the battle. Sadly, on that day, 30,000 Israeli foot soldiers were killed as well as the sons of Eli: Hophni and Phineas. The situation got worse. Besides the thousands of young men who were killed, the ark of the covenant was also taken.

THE ARK TRAVELS TO PHILISTIA

In the past, when the ark was out in front, the Israelites won their battles. The Philistines also reasoned that if they had the Ark, they would win all their battles, so they decided to take it.

Well, as the story goes, the journey of the ark in the land of the Philistines was not a very good adventure for the Philistines. Everywhere the Philistines took the ark, very bad things happened. Once they captured the ark, they tried to store it in several different cities, but everywhere it traveled, problems, famines, and pestilence followed. Finally, they put it in the temple of their god, Dagon, but when they came back the next morning, the image of Dagon had toppled on its face. When the priests saw this, they decided that a gust of wind must have blown it over, or something came in and knocked it down. They stood the image up again but the next morning it was knocked over again, and its head and hands were broken off.

The Philistine priests didn't know that it was because the ark was there, so for seven months, they moved it from place to place. Soon, nobody wanted it close to them. I can understand why. Wherever it was, the people began to get tumors all over their bodies, and rats began to infest the land.

They finally decided that they had had enough. "Let's get this thing back to Israel." They didn't want it around, but they didn't want to give it back. Was God behind the calamities, or was all this just happening by chance? They had to know for sure—but how? The Philistine leaders called on their "holy" men and asked them what to do. Their response:

> "...get a new cart ready, with two cows that have calved and have never been yoked. Hitch the cows to the cart, but take their calves away and pen them up. Take the ark of the Lord and put it on the cart, and in a chest beside it put the gold objects you are sending back to Him as a guilt offering. Send it on its way, but keep watching it. If it goes up to its own territory, toward Beth Shemesh, then the Lord has brought this great disaster on us. But if it does not, then we will know that it was not His hand that struck us and that it happened to us by chance."
>
> So they did this. They took two such cows and hitched them to the cart and penned up their calves. They placed the ark of the

Lord on the cart and along with it the chest containing the gold rats and the models of the tumors. **Then the cows went straight up toward Beth Shemesh, keeping on the road and lowing all the way; they did not turn to the right or to the left.** *The rulers of the Philistines followed them as far as the border of Beth Shemesh* (1 Sam. 6:7-12, NIV).

THE ARK RETURNS TO ISRAEL

The priests said to build a cart made out of new wood and then place the ark on the cart. They yoked two nursing cows to the cart but removed their calves and put them in pens. They knew that, if they released the cows and the cows tried to find their babies, then the ark was not causing the problem, because it would be simple maternal instinct that would drive them back to their young. However, if the cows took off without trying to find their calves, then that would not be natural.

When the cows were released, the Bible says they went straight on the road to Beth Shemesh, the opposite direction from where the calves were. Scripture says that, as they went, they went lowing. The cows did not want to go in the direction they were going. They wanted to go back and take care of their babies; they wanted to do what came natural to them. But there was something greater than instinct driving them—in the back seat on that cart was the presence of God directing them back to Israel.

CONSTRAINED BY THE PRESENCE OF GOD

We are like those cows; we want to do what comes natural to us. Every man and woman is bent on following the direction of his or her own will. Proverbs 16:9a says, "In his heart a man plans his course." The natural tendency of man is to go where he thinks it is best to go and to do what he thinks is best, even if it isn't. However, in God's presence, everything changes. The will of man is conquered by the will of God. The Lord's presence creates an irresistible draw in which man is now pushed in a direction he would not normally want to go. This isn't mind control or some kind of spiritual hocus-pocus; it's simply the enticing presence of God. God's presence is the vortex of spiritual power that draws the hungry heart into its divine current, where God then writes His will upon the human heart.

Remember how the pagan prophet Balaam was paid to prophesy doom against the Israelites, but was constrained from doing so by the presence of the Lord? (see Num. 22) Even though his employers promised great gain, he would not prophesy a negative word against Israel. He just couldn't get those words out of his mouth.

Often, people find themselves in situations much like the cows of Philistia or Balaam, the pagan prophet. They are doing what they think is best, but when they are suddenly thrust into the presence of the Lord, they are propelled into doing something else. They sense an irresistible draw to another action, and find no compelling reason not to resist that imposing divine will. Then, they become an instrument in the hand of God to bring about His purpose and plan on the earth. *If you will live in His presence, you will be drawn into His purposes for your life.*

GOD'S PRESENCE SUBORDINATES OUR PLANS TO HIS PLANS

Have you ever found yourself in that situation? Has God so moved in your life that your plans were altered by His presence? That is how we must live our lives. Our wills and desires must be subordinated to the will of the Father. Earlier, we discussed Proverbs 16:9. The second part of that verse states, "but the Lord determines his steps" (NIV).

It's okay to have a plan. It's okay to look at your future and determine what course you want to take. What is important, however, is to let God direct your steps. The Lord will give you a vision for your life. Remember, though, He knows the best way to bring it to pass. All things must be held loosely so that, at any moment, if God should direct, you are able to just move.

I have a vision for Metro Ministries. God has birthed in me a passion and vision for what I should do in New York. It's important for me to remember, though, that He is in charge. He's the one who directs the steps I take and the moves I make. He is the one who takes this thing that nobody else has done and turns it into a powerful, life-giving machine that feeds hungry souls.

All the energy behind what I do is the energy of God. I would have been dead long ago if it weren't for God. I've been beaten, shot, hit with a brick, had heart attacks, had tuberculosis—you name it, I've been there. If it was up to me, I would have gone another way, but His presence is what propels me.

GOD'S WAY ISN'T THE EASY WAY

Often we are reluctant servants, always looking for the easy way. Change is not easy. Our personal opinions and personal ambitions will often fight against the way that God wants to take us. But we must allow Him to etch His will upon the linings of our soul so that our hearts learn to beat in rhythm with the sound of Father's feet, taking us in the direction that He has for our lives. For His presence to prevail, we must leave the calves in the pen and go, lowing if necessary, in another direction. We cry, we scream, we holler, we complain, but God keeps calling. He is more committed to our ultimate good than we are, and He will find a way to get us to the place ordained for us. God is patient. He understands that we don't see the whole picture at once, so He patiently leads us on, helping us overcome our self-will and ignorance. Are you willing to move God's way, in His timing and not your own?

ARE YOU WILLING TO OBEY GOD'S NEXT COMMAND?

Are you ready to go, even lowing all the way—meaning that God is taking you in the complete opposite direction of where you wanted to go? When you are in the presence of God, sometimes you are moved in a direction that you would not have chosen. Sometimes the presence of God takes you in a direction you don't want to go, and you'll go lowing. You won't understand it—you'll wish it was different—"But He gives a greater grace. Therefore it says, 'God is opposed to the proud, but gives grace to the humble'" (James 4:6, NASB).

If you commit yourself to remain in God's presence, He will change you, move you, guide you, and make a way so that you can fulfill your divine destiny. As you learn to live in that presence, it will become a witness to those around you. The world witnesses, even if it does not understand, that another "government" is present when it sees ordinary men and women voluntarily choose to lay aside their own plans and choices to walk in joyful obedience to their God.

THE NEXT STEP MAY BE A DIFFERENT STEP

Remember that God's next step for you in life may be the exact opposite of the last step. God told Abraham and Sarah to have a baby. You know the story. At first, they tried to fulfill their dream through their own human ingenuity. Sarah sent Hagar to Abraham to have a baby. Ishmael was born. But Ishmael was a human plan, not God's plan. In the end, they finally obeyed God, and Isaac was born.

Many years later, when Isaac was older, God told Abraham to sacrifice Isaac. Abraham obeyed and put his precious son, Isaac, on the altar of sacrifice. But wait! Then God tells Abraham *not* to kill Isaac. God is testing Abraham's obedience and love. Life is full of twists and turns, tests and temptations. Your response in the time of testing will determine the measure of character that has been built into your life. The tests don't build character; they reveal character. Are you willing to obey the next step God commands you to take even if it's the exact opposite of the last step He commanded you?

As the cows went, they went lowing, because it was the total opposite of what they wanted to do, what they should have done, even against their natural instinct. There have been many days in my life when I've gone lowing. Nevertheless, when you're in God's presence, you'll automatically find His purpose. Because you're close enough to Him, His presence just moves you.

LIFE PRINCIPLES IN THE CROSSHAIRS:

- **The Lord's presence creates an irresistible draw in which man now wants to go where He wants to go and do what He wants to do.**

- **All things must be held loosely so that, at any moment, if God should speak, you are able to just say "yes."**

- **"Lowing" is the proper position for the servant of God. It is the position that brings the grace of God into your life.**

- **Obey God's *next step* for you, even it's the opposite of what you expect.**

In His presence, you will be changed and the change will continue for the rest of your life. Life is about change, as we are being reconstructed into His image. This process is only possible for those who choose to remain in His presence.

—Bill Wilson

In the presence of Your infinite might,
I'm so small and frail and weak.
When I see Your power and wisdom, Lord
I have no words left to speak.
In the presence of a holy God
There's new meaning now to grace.
You took all my sins upon Yourself.
I can only stand amazed.

—Mark Altroggel

God wills that we should push on into His Presence and live our whole life there. This is to be known to us in conscious experience. It is more than a doctrine to be held, it is a life to be enjoyed every moment of every day.

—A. W. Tozer

Chapter 20

The Power of His Presence Creates a Pursuit of His Presence

So David and the elders of Israel and the commanders of units of a thousand went to bring up the ark of the covenant of the Lord from the house of Obed-Edom, with rejoicing (1 Chron. 15:25, NIV).

This principle, concerning the presence of God and the purpose of God, is one that has the capacity to alter the way you live, if you let it. When the right principles are applied to your life, they have the power to rearrange your thoughts and actions in a way that can positively change the course of your life. As we look at the story of Obed-Edom, attempt to visualize yourself in his place, and see if you can determine what inner motivations were compelling this amazing man to make the kind of commitment he made. This is a crucial issue—what motivates a person to take action in the face of opportunity or in the presence of trouble? What makes a man or woman step out of the mainstream of mediocrity in order to take action in a time of adversity? The life of Obed-Edom will give us some clues to these questions.

When the ark of the covenant was stolen in battle, it ended up in the hands of the Philistines for twenty years (see 1 Sam. 7:2). When David came into power, one of the first things that he wanted to do was to bring it back to Jerusalem. David understood the spiritual significance of the ark and longed to have the awesome presence of God once again in its proper place, in the Holy of Holies, in the Tabernacle. David was a man who loved the Presence and would make any sacrifice to get its symbol back. His spiritual priorities were certainly clear and were established early in his reign as the king of Israel.

Once the ark was finally back in the land of Israel, a tragedy struck. Because they were so anxious to get the ark back, they did not plan according to the divine plan given by God. Remember that you must do God's work according to His ways. After that false start, David decide to it the right way. He needed to find an appropriate place for the ark while the plans were being worked out for a festival to celebrate the return of the presence of God. The preparations for this festival were enormous and would take nearly three months, which meant that David had to do something with the ark until they were ready for its return to Jerusalem. Where do you put the ark of the covenant for three months? Maybe we could ask it like this, "Where do you put the presence of God for three months while preparing for this celebration?"

THE ARK AND OBED-EDOM

David chose a man's home, strangely enough, in which to put the Ark. Obed-Eedom, the man who was chosen, is a rather obscure biblical character. *Obed-Edom* means "servant of Edom"; and we know that he was a Gittite, which means that he was an inhabitant of Gath. Edomites were descendants of Esau; and Gath, you might remember, was the city Goliath came from. Gath was the city where David hid from Saul, who was seeking to take his life.

All that is really known about Obed-Edom is that, for three months the ark of God was in his house. The presence of God was made resident in the home of a descendant of Esau. What a powerful truth lies behind this fact. As with Rahab the harlot, the grace of God extends itself to the very least among us. No matter where you are born or where you have come from, God's presence is available to you. This is the mystery and miracle of God's grace.

Way back, during Israel's journey through the wilderness on their way to the Promised Land, there were a couple of clans whose responsibility it was to move the Tabernacle. One of those was Merari, a son of Levi. He was responsible for the structure that held the whole thing together, the framework. It is believed that Obed-Edom was a Merarite Levite. We see his name again in First Chronicles 15:18, where he is a gatekeeper. In First Chronicles 15:21, he would be in the transport party of the Ark, and was to be a harp player in the celebration. In First Chronicles 15:24, he would be a guard of the ark with Elkanah, and further in First Chronicles, we see that even Obed-Edom's family was so blessed that they, too, wanted more and more to serve the Lord.

We do not know where, in his house, Obed-Edom put the ark. I have a feeling that it was most certainly positioned in a place of honor. It would be natural for you to wonder what there was about this man that made him an acceptable choice by King David for housing and protecting the most famous piece of furniture in the history of Israel. In the preparations being made for the coming celebration of the return of the lost ark, we will discover a few clues that will help us peek into the heart of this man.

As we realize Obed-Edom's passion, we will also discover some powerful principles that we can apply to our own lives. First Chronicles 15 lists the volunteers who offered themselves to make the preparations for this festival. There were musicians, singers, gatekeepers, and ministers. It's interesting to note that Obed-Edom volunteered to serve in every one of these positions. We will discover some timeless truths that some Christians today may find a bit unsettling. Here was a man who had a passion for the Presence and was willing to make great personal sacrifice to be as close as he could to the presence of God. His passion and priorities stand as a great testimony to his life and are an example for all of us.

THEY NEEDED SINGERS

In First Chronicles 15:16-18 we see that Obed-Edom was part of the worship team leading the parade of bringing back the ark. The presence of God had produced a song in his heart and inspired him to worship. With his harp, he created a melody of worship that resonated strongly during the procession.

First Chronicles 15:24 goes on to say that Obed-Edom was among the gatekeepers of the Ark. The gatekeepers were those who had such an experience of the riches of God's presence that they devoted their whole lives to ushering others into the presence of God. To hear another account of this, read Psalm 84, paying special attention to verse 10.

THEY NEEDED GATEKEEPERS

First Chronicles 15:24 mentions that Obed-Edom was a gatekeeper of the Ark. The gatekeepers formed a large sacred order from the time of David (see 1 Chron. 9:22; 23:5). Their duties and the words describing them in two passages, "keepers of the thresholds" (see 1 Chron. 9:19) and "porters of the thresholds" (see 2 Chron. 23:4), connect them in some measure with the "keeper of the threshold" referred to above. They guarded the gates of the house of Yahweh (see 1 Chron. 9:23), closing and opening them at the proper times (see 1 Chron. 9:27), and preventing the unclean from entering the sacred enclosure (see 2 Chron. 23:19). They had charge of the sacred vessels and of the free-will offerings (see 2 Chron. 31:14), and dwelt in the chambers about the temple (see 1 Chron. 9:27). They were Levites, and came in from the Levitical villages every seventh day for service in their turn (see 1 Chron. 9:25). Their office was honorable, ranking with the singers, after the priests and Levites (see Ezra 2:42; 1 Chron. 15:18). Obed-Edom was part of this sacred order of Levitical priests who guarded the entryways into the most holy places of the Tabernacle.

THEY NEEDED MINISTERS

> *He appointed some of the Levites **as** ministers before the ark of the Lord, even to celebrate and to thank and praise the Lord God of Israel: Asaph the chief, and second to him Zechariah, then Jeiel, Shemiramoth, Jehiel, Mattithiah, Eliab, Benaiah, Obed-edom, and Jeiel, with musical instruments, harps, lyres; also Asaph played loud-sounding cymbals* (1 Chron. 16:4-5, NASB).

Obed-Edom is selected as a minister before the ark to celebrate, to thank and to praise the Lord God. Everywhere you turn, Obed-Edom is right in the middle of worship, ministry, and guarding the entryways to the Tabernacle. He is a man who has become obsessed with the presence of God, and his one desire is to be near the place of His presence. It rather sounds like David's words in Psalm 27:4: "One thing I have asked from the Lord, that I shall seek: That I may dwell in the house of the Lord all the days of my life, to behold the beauty of the Lord, and to meditate in His temple" (NASB).

So, where do you find people like Obed-Edom? Why was he so willing to serve in all aspects of the worship of the people? What were his motivations? It was the impact that the presence of God made on his life. It's all about the presence of God. Remember, the ark had not even been removed from his house yet. Can you imagine being in such close proximity to the manifest presence of God for three months?

Could it be that, during the three months Obed-Edom had the manifest presence of God in his house, something happened to him? He determined that if they needed help, whatever it was, he would do it. Obed-Edom knew that he would never have the ark in his house like that again, so he volunteered to serve as a door-keeper. Then, he could stand right there, at the edge of the door, as close to the ark as he could get, as close to the presence of God as possible. He would gladly stand there for eight hours because he remembered what it was like when the ark was in his house in the next room!

GOD'S PRESENCE CHANGES YOU

Once you've been in God's presence, folks, everything changes. Why do you think we go through all the contortions we do in New York to get kids to Sunday school? Why do you think pastors always encourage you to be in church? It's because we know that, if we can get people into the presence of God just one time, they may have an experience they would never have otherwise.

When I was picked up off the street, I was just a boy. The man who took me in had no idea what God would do in my life. When I showed up at youth camp, the first time I had ever been to church in my life, he knew that, if he could get me into the presence of God just one time, something would happen. Nobody wanted to pray with me because my clothes were old and dirty. Nobody wanted to have anything to do with me because I didn't look like the rest of the kids. But that night, when I responded to the invitation, something happened to me. I experienced something that I had never experienced in my entire life. I knew that night that something had happened, and that experience is as real today as it was all those years ago. What happened? I got into the presence of God, and it made a difference.

Where did the zeal of Obed-Edom come from? We don't know what, but something happened to him in the presence of God. I wonder what would happen to you if you had the presence of God in your house for three months. I wonder how your relationships would change. I wonder how your kids would be. I wonder how the whole countenance of your family would be. For three months, Obed-Edom had the presence of God in his house. Afterward, whatever it took, he was there.

Obed-Edom said, "Let me stand next to the door. If that's all I can do, then that's all I'll do." He said, "I can do that. I can help. You need any help, preacher? Do you need somebody to run errands? Do you need someone to be picked up at the airport? Do you need somebody to clean the building? Do you need somebody to watch the nursery?"

MOVED TO ACT BY HIS PRESENCE

I never had any birthday parties in my life, until just recently. I usually shy away from all the hoopla, but a church I was in decided to throw one for me. They went all out with the cake, ice cream, and cards—the whole meal deal. As it was winding down, I hung around and was just staring at the last piece of cake, thinking.

During this whole thing, there was an old lady in her seventies that had been standing off to the side. She had on a pink and white flowered dress, very old, ripped, kind of torn and frayed. She hadn't eaten anything, she'd just been watching. She waited until everyone was gone and then came over to me. So, I'm sitting there, looking at this last piece of cake like an idiot and, you know, meditating on the cake. Her hand was in a closed fist and was shaking like she had Parkinson's disease.

The old woman said, "I have nothing, but what I have left I want to give to you. I want you to use this to buy a Christmas present for a little boy that was like you when you were little. You buy that little boy a present and you tell him that somebody loves him." I was struggling a bit and I didn't know quite what to do. "Hold out your hand," she said. I did and she opened her fist. In her hand was thirty-five cents—a quarter and a dime. "This is all I have, but you use this to help buy a present for a little boy like you." I'm sure that you have been in spots like this where everything goes into slow motion. I asked her why she was doing this. She said, "I felt a presence in the service this morning that I have never felt that way in my entire life. I must do something with it."

There it is. When you get in the presence of God, things change. More importantly, we are changed in His presence.

Why do I do what I do? Why do I still drive the bus? Why do I still go out and grind through all the mess and hassle? Because I remember what it felt like when I came forward at the age of 16. I was in the presence of God. Even as a boy, I recognized it had to be God. Though I didn't understand what was going on, didn't know all the right religious terms, didn't know how to raise my hands, or even how to say "God bless you" on cue, I knew it was God. I didn't know any of that. All I knew was that my mom didn't want me and I was hungry. But when I came to the altar that night, something happened to me. It was not a bolt of lightning. I didn't hear voices, I didn't get knocked off my donkey, but I felt something. I experienced something. The man who picked me up was repeatedly asked why he did it. He answered, "I thought that if I could just get the boy into the presence of God one time, maybe something would happen." I guess it did, didn't it? That's been a long time ago, but it's still just as real today.

Once you've been in His presence, everything changes. The old missionary told me, "If you're going to make it, don't ever leave the presence of God." In His presence, you will be changed, and the change will continue for the rest of your life. Life is about change, since we are being reconstructed into His image. This process is only possible for those who choose to remain in His presence.

Are you willing to abide in His presence?

Hearts that are "fit to break" with love for the Godhead are those who have been in the Presence and have looked with opened eye upon the majesty of Deity. Men of the breaking hearts had a quality about them not known or understood by common men.[1]

You will be uncomfortable. What you expect will rarely happen the way you expect it. God will always do something new in your life (see Isa. 43:18-19). But believe me, staying in His presence will give you the power to do whatever He requires of you.

LIFE PRINCIPLES IN THE CROSSHAIRS:

- **Don't leave God's presence.**
- **Expect to be changed in His presence.**
- **In God's presence, you will discover your purpose.**
- **God is doing something new in and through you. Be ready for the new thing that is about to hit your life.**

FINAL WORDS

These twenty principles of life and leadership are far from an exhaustive list of what you need to know in order to be equipped. However, they are a start. You must start somewhere and sometime. Why not now, right where you are?

Implement these principles. Decide here and now to stay in God's presence. Be a willing servant, obeying His next command.

God's Spirit will give you the power and the willingness to move forward if you surrender. Let go of your old, ineffective ways. Release the past; grasp God's new thing in your life.

I want to pray for you:

Lord, give this reader the courage to let go of the past and the willingness to walk in Your new ways and directions. I pray that God will help you receive truth in love and to be open to confrontation and correction. I ask God to send faithful and truthful friends around you to pray for you and help you see the blind spots in your life. Most of all, I pray that you will never leave God's presence. In Jesus' mighty name, Amen.

ENDNOTES

CHAPTER 1

1. Savage, Robert. Qtd. in "Browse Authors" (Online). <http://www.worldofquotes.com/author/Robert-C.-Savage/1/index.html>

2. Rumsfeld, Donald. Qtd. in "Donald Rumsfeld Quotes" (Online). <http://en.thinkexist.com/quotes/donald_rumsfeld/2.html>

3. Reagan, Ronald. Qtd. in "Determination Quotes." Your Guide to Quotations (Online, Simran Khurana). <http://quotations.about.com/cs/inspirationquotes/a/Determination3.htm>

4. Lombardi, Vince. Qtd. in "Vince Lombardi Quotes" (Online). <http://www.brainyquote.com/quotes/quotes/v/vincelomba125250.html>

CHAPTER 2

1. Parker, Dorothy. Qtd. in "The Quotations Page" (Online). <http://www.quotationspage.com/subjects/money/>

2. Clarke, James Freeman. Qtd. in "Great-Quotes.com" (Online). <http://www.great-quotes.com/faith_quotes.htm>

3. Chambers, Oswald. Qtd. in "Great-Quotes.com" (Online). <http://www.great-quotes.com/faith_quotes.htm>

4. Parker, Dorothy. Qtd. in "The Quotations Page" (Online). <http://www.quotationspage.com/subjects/money/>

5. Chambers, Oswald. Qtd. in "Great-Quotes.com" (Online). <http://www.great-quotes.com/faith_quotes.htm>

CHAPTER 3

1. <http://www.wisdomquotes.com/cat_sacrifice.html>

2. Bryan, William Jennings. Qtd. in "William Jennings Bryan Quotes" (Online). <http://en.thinkexist.com/quotes/william_jennings_bryan/>

3. Beecher, Henry Ward. Qtd. in "Motivational Quotations—Helping Others" (Online). <http://www.wow4u.com/helping/ >

CHAPTER 4

1. King, Jr., Martin Luther. Qtd. in "Quotable Quotes" (Online, Chris Fox). <http://www.chrisfoxinc.com/quotableQuotes.htm>

2. Churchill, Winston. Qtd. in "Inspirational and Quotable Quotes" (Online). <http://www.albertarose.org/Interest/Quotes.html>

3. Keller, Helen. Qtd. in "The Quoteboard: Optimism Quotes" (Online). <http://www.thequoteboard.com/categoryquotes.php?category=Optimism&categoryid=257>

4. Ps. 1:1, NASB

5. Anonymous.   <http://www.quotelady.com/subjects/perseverance.html>

6. Churchill, Winston. Qtd. in "Inspirational and Quotable Quotes" (Online). <http://www.albertarose.org/Interest/Quotes.html>

CHAPTER 5

1, Allen, George Herbert. Qtd. in _____ (Online). <http://www.quoteworld.org/browse.php?thetext=quit,give+up,give+in,giving+up,giving+in>

2. Da Vinci, Leonardo. Qtd. in "Motivational and Inspirational Corner...America's System for Success" (Online). <http://www.motivational-inspirational-corner.com/getquote.html?categoryid=10>

3. *Christian History Magazine* Vol. 16, 1997, pg. 12.

CHAPTER 6

1. Romans 1:14, NASB

2. Washington, Booker T. Qtd. in "Opposition" (Online). <http://www.quotelady.com/subjects/opposition.html>

CHAPTER 7

1. Bell, Alexander Graham. Qtd. in "Daily Inspiring Quotes: Determination" (Online). <http://www.dailyinspiringquotes.com/deter2.shtml>

Chapter 16

1. Lawrence, Brother. *The Practice of the Presence of God: The Best Rule of Holy Life.* Grand Rapids. Christian Classics Ethereal Library. Public Domain. 15 Mar. 2001. Online. <http://www.ccel.org/ccel/lawrence/practice.all.html>

Chapter 20

1. Tozer, A.W. "Chapter 3: Removing the Veil." A Pursuit of God. Online.<http://calvarychapel.com/library/Tozer-AW/Pursuit OfGod/03.htm>

BIBLIOGRAPHY

Allen, George Herbert. Qtd. in _____ . (Online). <http://www.quoteworld.org/browse.php?thetext= quit,give+up,give+in,giving+up,giving+in>.

Altrogge, Mark. "In The Presence." Qtd. in "In Christ Alone! Dedicated to the Proclamation of Jesus Christ" (Online). 23 Aug. 2004. < http://www.inchristalone.org/InThePresence.html>.

Anonymous. Qtd. in "My Favorite Future's Quotes and More" (Online). <http://www.passig.com/pic/My%20Future's%20 Quotes.htm>.

Anonymous. Qtd. in "My Favorite Future's Quotes and More" (Online). <http://www.passig.com/pic/My%20Future's%20 Quotes.htm>.

Beecher, Henry Ward. Qtd. in "From Wisdom Quotes: Quotations to Inspire and Challenge" (Online, Jone Johnson Lewis). <http://www.wisdomquotes.com/cat_friendship.html>.

Beecher, Henry Ward. Qtd. in "Motivational Quotations—Helping Others" (Online). <http://www.wow4u.com/helping/>.

Bell, Alexander Graham. Qtd. in "Daily Inspiring Quotes: Determination" (Online).<http://www.dailyinspiringquotes.com/ deter2.shtml>.

Bell, Alexander Graham. Qtd in _____ . (Online). <http://www.quoteworld.org/browse.php?thetext= quit,give+up,give+in,giving+up,giving+in>.

Bonhoeffer, Dietrich. Qtd. in "Amindra: Wisdom of the Mind and Soul" (Online) <http://koti.mbnet.fi/amindra/decchar1. htm>.

Bonhoeffer, Dietrich. Qtd. in "Motivational and Inspirational Corner...America's System for Success" (Online). <http://www. motivational-inspirational-corner.com/getquote.html? categoryid=43>.

Buck, Pearl. Qtd. in "The Quotations Page" (Online). <http://www.quotationspage.com/subjects/mistakes/21. html>.

Bush, George H. Qtd. in "Leading Thoughts: Building a Community of Leaders" (Online). <http://www.leadershipnow. com/leadershipquotes.html>.

Chambers, Oswald. Qtd. in "Great-Quotes.com" (Online). <http://www.great-quotes.com/faith_quotes.htm>.

Christian History Magazine. Vol. 16. 1997. 12.

Churchill, Winston. Qtd. in "Inspirational and Quotable Quotes" (Online). <http://www.albertarose.org/Interest/Quotes. html>.

Clarke, James Freeman. Qtd. in "Great-Quotes.com" (Online). <http://www.great-quotes.com/faith_quotes.htm>.

Da Vinci, Leonardo. Qtd. in "Motivational and Inspirational Corner…America's System for Success" (Online). <http://www.motivational-inspirational-corner.com/ getquote.html?categoryid=10>.

Demosthenes. Qtd. in "The Quotations Page" (Online). <http://www.quotationspage.com/subjects/opportunity/>.

Drummond, Henry. Qtd. in "The Alchemy of Influence" (Online). <http://www.ccel.org/d/drummond/greatest/htm/v.iii. htm>.

Edison, Thomas A. Qtd. in "The Quotations Page" (Online). <http://www.quotationspage.com/subjects/opportunity/>.

Elliot, L.G. Qtd. in "Motivational and Inspirational Corner…America's System for Success" (Online). <http://www.motivational-inspirational-corner.com/ getquote.html?startrow=11&categoryid=61>.

Emerson, Ralph Waldo. Qtd. in "Motivational and Inspirational Corner…America's System for Success" (Online). <http://www.motivational-inspirational-corner.com/ getquote.html?categoryid=17>.

Evans, Melvin J. Qtd. in "Famous Quotes by Melvin J. Evans." (Online). <http://www.zaadz.com/quotes/authors/melvin _j_evans>.

Fosdick, Harry. Qtd. in "Famous Quotes About Bitterness" (Online). <http://www.zaadz.com/quotes/topics/bitterness/ ?page=5>.

Keller, Helen. Qtd. in "Indian Child Faith Quotes" (Online). <http://www.indianchild.com/Quotes/faith_quotes.htm>.

Keller, Helen. Qtd. in "Helen Keller Quotes" (Online). <http://www.thinkexist.com/English/Author/x/Author_3057_2.htm>.

Keller, Helen. Qtd. in "The Quoteboard: Optimism Quotes" (Online). <http://www.thequoteboard.com/categoryquotes.php?category=Optimism&categoryid=257>.

King, Jr., Martin Luther. Qtd. in "Indian Child Faith Quotes" (Online). <http://www.indianchild.com/Quotes/faith_quotes.htm>.

King, Jr., Martin Luther. Qtd. in "Quotable Quotes" (Online, Chris Fox). <http://www.chrisfoxinc.com/quotableQuotes.htm>.

Landers, Ann. Qtd. in "Famous Quotes with Resentment" (Online). <http://en.thinkexist.com/keyword/resentment/>.

Lawrence, Brother. The Practice of the Presence of God: The Best Rule of Holy Life. Grand Rapids. Christian Classics Ethereal Library. Public Domain. 15 Mar. 2001. Online. <http://www.ccel.org/ccel/lawrence/practice.all.html>.

Lincoln, Abraham. Qtd. in "Resources—Quotes: Responsibility, Duty" (Online, Josephson Institute of Ethics). <http://www.josephsoninstitute.org/quotes/quoteresponsibility.htm>.

Lombardi, Vince. Qtd. in "Vince Lombardi Quotes" (Online). <http://www.brainyquote.com/quotes/quotes/v/vincelomba125250.html>.

MacDonald, Gordon. Qtd. in "Empowered Leaders." Character (Online, by Hans Finzel). <http://www.wowi.net/cgi-bin/article_list.cgi?command=view&id=679>.

Newton, John. <http:// psalm121.ca/quotes/dcqnewton.html>.)

Nin, Anais. Qtd. in "Change/Growth Quotes: From Wisdom Quotes" (Online, Jone Johnson Lewis). <http://www.wisdomquotes.com/cat_changegrowth.html>.

Parker, Dorothy. Qtd. in "The Quotations Page" (Online). <http://www.quotationspage.com/subjects/money/>.

Perot, H. Ross. Qtd. in "Browse Topics: Quitting" (Online). <http://www.worldofquotes.com/topic/Quitting/1/>.

Reagan, Ronald. Qtd. in "Determination Quotes." Your Guide to Quotations (Online, Simran Khurana). <http://quotations.about.com/cs/inspirationquotes/a/Determination3.htm>.

Rockefeller, Jr., John D. Qtd. in "Responsibility" (Online). <http://www.quotelady.com/subjects/responsibility.html>.

Roosevelt, Eleanor. Qtd. in "Favorite Quotes (Online). <http://www.geocities.com/Heartland/Bluffs/8104/quotes/new. html>.

Roosevelt, Theodore. Qtd. in "Sacrifice Quotes: From Wisdom Quotes to Inspire and Challenge" (Online, Jone Johnson Lewis). <http://www.wisdomquotes.com/cat_sacrifice. html>.

Rumsfeld, Donald. Qtd. in "Donald Rumsfeld Quotes" (Online). <http://en.thinkexist.com/quotes/donald_rumsfeld/2.html>.

Savage, Robert. Qtd. in "Browse Authors" (Online). <http://www.worldofquotes.com/author/Robert-C.-Savage/1/>.

Schweitzer, Albert. Qtd. in "Energize…Especially for Leaders of Volunteers: Quotes" (Online, submitted by Deborah Stroup). <http://www.energizeinc.com/reflect/quote1.html>.

Smedes, Lewis B. Shame and Grace. New York: Harper Collins. 1993. 3.

Steele, Shelby. Qtd. in "Freedom's Nest Quotes: Quotes on Victims" (Online). <http://www.freedomsnest.com/cgi-bin/q.cgi?subject=victims>.

Tozer, A.W. "Chapter 5: the Universal Presence." The Pursuit of God. Online. <http://www.sendrevival.com/pioneers/aw-tozer/The_Pursuit_of_God/chapter_5.htm>.

Tozer, A.W. "Chapter 3: Removing the Veil." A Pursuit of God. Online. <http://calvarychapel.com/library/Tozer-AW/Pursuit OfGod/03.htm>.

Tozer, A.W. Qtd. in "A.W. Tozer Quotes" (Online). 2002. <http://home.earthlink.net/~covenantcomputing/sealed/AWTozer.htm>.

Tozer, A.W. Qtd. in "World of Quotes" (Online). <http://www.worldofquotes.com/author/A.-W.-Tozer/1/>.

Washington, Booker T. Qtd. in "Opposition" (Online). <http://www.quotelady.com/subjects/opposition.html>.

Wilder, Thornton. Qtd. in "The Quote Cache" (Online). <http://quotes.prolix.nu/Authors/?Thornton_Wilder>.

INTRODUCE A CHILD TO JESUS
WON-BY-ONE
CHILD SPONSORSHIP PROGRAM

Where would you be if no one ever told you about Jesus?

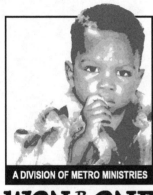

A DIVISION OF METRO MINISTRIES

WON ᴮ/ᵧ ONE

You can fulfill the Great Commission and introduce an at-risk child to Jesus by partnering with Metro Ministries through our monthly child sponsorship program, **Won-By-One**.

Every child should know that he or she was created with purpose, is not a mistake, and is loved by God. You might not live in Brooklyn, or near the garbage dumps outside of Manila, but you can still share the love of Jesus every week with a child who does live there. Your financial commitment of $23 a month will make sure a child whom you may never meet participates in Sunday School, receives home visits and gets a chance to know the love of their Heavenly Father.

More importantly, the sponsored child receives prayer and encouragement from someone outside of their environment who cares about his or her life and soul. As a sponsor, you will receive a packet and picture of your child along with periodic updates, including letters from your child. You can be involved as much and as long as you want. All monies, gifts and correspondence are processed through Metro Ministries, and your personal information is kept confidential.

**Make a difference today and introduce a child to Jesus.
They are waiting.**

To become a **Won-By-One** partner or receive more information, please go to our web site, www.metroministries.org, or call toll free 1-877-WON BY ONE (966-2966).

ELEMENTS of RELEVANCE

If you enjoyed this book, you will love the *Elements of Relevance* leadership training series.

Leaders aren't born; they're made.

With the monthly training series *Elements of Relevance*, you and your leadership team can join Pastor Bill Wilson every month in his staff meetings. Through this monthly training series, Pastor Bill will give you both the spiritual and practical tools you need to impart the key principles in developing leadership for effective ministry. *Elements of Relevance—Principles of Life and Leadership* is a monthly training series that is perfect for individual study, church and ministry staff meetings, Sunday School or study groups, and leadership and lay training.

You'll impart to your leadership the ministry keys to:

Motivation	Relationship building
Loyalty	Servanthood
Excellence	Longevity
Communication skills	Vision
Encouragement	Proactive leaders
Faithfulness	Biblical truths
Conflict resolution	Finding leaders
Evaluating personnel	Growth

To sign up or for more information, go to Metro's website
www.metroministries.org.

Develop a Sidewalk/Indoor
Sunday School in your neighborhood!!

Directly from the most duplicated children's ministry in the world comes the most comprehensive, original, affordable, and easy-to-use children's material available!

"I have always wanted to take the methods, stories, and teaching principles that we use here in NY and around the world, and make it available to everyone! They will transform your classroom, but more importantly, they will transform your children."
—Bill Wilson, Founder and Senior Pastor of Metro Ministries

Training Today's Timothys

This is a perfect book for anyone interested in starting a Sidewalk Sunday School site. Not only is this book easy to read, but it gives you step-by-step instructions on how to start a site from scratch, put a team together, plan a lesson, communicate with your audience, dismiss the kids and conduct your first home visit. This manual has hundreds of tips and secrets used by our staff members here on the streets of New York City and others from all over the world who have taken our model of Sunday School back to their countries and are now reaching their communities. Metro Ministries is the most duplicated ministry in the world because it is built on principles, not personalities. These principles have been tried and proven for nearly 40 years. *Training Today's Timothys* is our way of sharing with you an effective soul-winning ministry that works.

Book of Worms - Flyers

Every week, our ministry makes over 20,000 home visits to kids who attend our Sunday School. We hand deliver advertisement flyers to the door of each child. Not only are the flyers the tools used to open the doors for us, they are also our signature cards. How your flyers look reflect your ministry. This book is a great resource tool to help you design flyers, use them to boost attendance, build a roster, as advertisement at elementary schools and to promote special events that occur at Sunday School. If you are interested in making home visits to the children who attend your Sunday School, you will need a tool to get you through the door. *Book of Worms – flyers* is a perfect place to start.

Children's Learning Curriculum

Absolutely the best, most comprehensive children's curriculum available, period. Each 13-week program (4 in all for a full year) is loaded with interactive material and step-by-step instructions that will help you as you teach your children basic biblical principles, as well as games, object lessons, and music. Written and based on the format used around the world by the Metro staff, this is all you need for Sunday School, midweek service, or a backyard Bible club.

Metro Ministries Resources

For more information on Pastor Bill's sermons, books, leadership training materials, or Christian Education resources, please visit the website www.metroministries.org. or call 1-800-791-8996

Metro Ministries
PO Box 370695
Brooklyn, NY 11237-0695

Pastor Bill Wilson

For Pastor Bill's ministry itinerary schedule or to contact his office for a speaking engagement or seminar, please contact his office at 718-453-3352, or e-mail us at: info@metroministries.com

Internship Program

Our mission is to equip individuals with the tools necessary to accomplish God's specific purpose for them in ministry. People come from all over the world to work with our staff for a semester, obtaining hands-on training in children's and youth ministry and outreach evangelism. Many interns have taken their new skills and implemented effective, new programs for ministry in their native countries.

Brooklyn Boot Camp

As America's largest Sunday School challenges itself to greater levels of urban outreach, it challenges you to make a decision. Are you ready to ride on the buses through a vast wasteland? Are you prepared to handle Sunday School sessions ministering to thousands of children?

An essential to long-term survival in urban ministry is the ability to work within a team. We get you ready with a tough-as-nails ropes training program. It will test and prepare you for the rigors of urban life. This is a life-changing program designed to train and equip you for sharing the gospel in the inner cities of the world.

To keep it real, we made it street-wise and street-tough.
It enables you to:
Gain firsthand experience for urban ministry.
Experience the principles behind what we do.
Take your experience to the streets of your city.
For more information, email us: bootcamp@metroministries.com
or call 718-453-3352.

Contact the website for more information
on either of the above programs.
www.metroministries.org

Additional copies of this book and other
book titles from DESTINY IMAGE are
available at your local bookstore.

For a complete list of our titles,
visit us at www.destinyimage.com
Send a request for a catalog to:

Destiny Image₍ₐ₎ Publishers, Inc.
P.O. Box 310
Shippensburg, PA 17257-0310

*"Speaking to the Purposes of God for This
Generation and for the Generations to Come"*